Donato Maniello

Augmented reality in public spaces

Basic techniques for video mapping

VOLUME I
New Technologies for the Arts

Le Penseur Publisher

Augmented reality in public spaces
Basic techniques for video mapping

VOLUME I
New Technologies for the Arts

by **Donato Maniello**

Original title: *Realtà aumentata in spazi pubblici – Tecniche base di video mapping*
© LE PENSEUR 2014

traslated by **Sarah Julia Ryan**

Images shown in this volume:

On the cover: Cloister of San Francesco, Palazzo di Città – Ostuni (BR), Italy. Location of the first GLOWFestival, 2013. The images at the beginning of each chapter are photos of the work by the gloWArp studio, which owns the rights. The images in Chapter 1, taken from material freely available online, were taken by the respective owners of whom it Is not possible to find references, and for which there was no specific guidance on the type of copyright. The images in the later chapters, except for screenshots, are the property of the gloWArp studio. The image locations shown in this volume, if not otherwise stated, are found in Italy.

Software used in this volume:

- Adobe Photoshop® CS6
- Adobe Illustrator® CS6
- Adobe Premiere® CS6
- Maxon Cinema 4D® R14
- Resolume Arena® 4.1.7
- Squared 5 MPEG Streamclip®

For software not indicated in this list, we recommend using the latest release available. All the software mentioned in this volume is the property of its respective software house which owns the copyright.

Chapters 3, 4 and 6 are by Luigi Console

Luigi Console, Graphic designer with a Masters degree in "Visual Design", directs his research on the connection between analogue and digital visual communication techniques. From 2012 to 2014 he has been part of the gloWArp studio. He is currently a freelance lecturer for workshops related to New Technologies for the Arts.

Font used in the book: Titillium, OFL licensed typeface designed during Campi Visivi's Type Design course - Academy of Fine Arts in Urbino – Italy

© LE PENSEUR
Via Monte Calvario, 40/3 – 85050 Brienza (PZ) – ITALY
ISBN 978-88-95315-34-8
1st edition: June 2015

In the event that any errors or inaccuracies are found in this volume, the publisher and author apologise and kindly request that you inform them in an email to info@lepenseur.it

To see our latest books visit our website: www.edizionilepenseur.it

INDEX

Chapter 10 – Procedure for implementing a video mapping event

by Donato Maniello

Foreword

Mapping is nothing more than the culmination of research that is rooted in the historical avant-garde and based on utopia – a concrete utopia – where you can escape from the rigid frame of the film screen, just as the Futurists had already gone beyond the borders of the painting frame, invading space.

After reaching the 90's, when it was thought that it should be the viewer to penetrate and interact in a virtual space, in the twenty-first century we realised it was simply necessary to expand the real space that we inhabit daily. Therefore it had to be virtual reality to integrate – through devices, reading information and viewing pictures – with the concrete reality, increasing it. The world has become primarily imaginative, to live in real time, not isolating it solipsistically and getting lost in other universes through a helmet and a dataglove (virtual reality), but sharing this journey into hyperspace with other people (augmented reality). That said, however, even the virtual dimension is now back in fashion, thanks to the new Sony device Morpheus©.

Moreover, the audiovisual technological evolution of the last two decades, while pushing us towards an individual and intimate vision through handheld devices, on the other hand has enhanced the possibility of creating a collective mega-vision, turning the facades of skyscrapers into screens (resulting in media buildings): so on one hand augmented reality unfolds itself in google glass, on the other it becomes a visually compelling mapping spectacle. And in all this the cinemas are not yet extinct and mass projections in enclosed spaces still, fortunately, continue to exist.

We should add that mapping, as well as realising the dream of the avant-garde and neo avant-garde, perfecting the concept of expanded cinema developed in the late '60s, becoming the culmination of cinema installations first and increasingly immersive video installations after, marks but a return to the past – as also clearly illustrated at the beginning of this book: to Renaissance perspective and to the great baroque machines based on optical and spacial illusion. The "breaking" of the avant-garde is never in contradiction to the base of the classical view, but it is rather an intensification.

Art has always set itself the goal of seducing and engaging, even perceptually, the viewer, and the phrase that the Futurists wrote in the Technical Manifesto of Painting in 1912, that "we will put the viewer at the centre of the picture," is a goal that artists were aiming at in the fifteenth, as well as in the seventeenth and twentieth centuries. The only difference is that today, thanks to new technologies, we can put it into practice how, where and when we want.

This volume has the merit, after a brief discussion of historical characteristics, of indicating methods and techniques to accomplish mapping, thus assuming the form of a manual, which is very detailed but also easy to read. What is now even more important, given the awareness and knowledge of the medium and the technologies supported by it, is that, as the first necessary stage to activate this creativity, through an art form so spectacular and full of visual possibilities, artists must look within themselves.

It is, of course, essential to have a premise and give ideas to the reader-creator of images from this book that will take technical and aesthetic cues. It is not advisable to consider technology like the ring of King Midas, as the solution to all problems. Technology without imagination is useless. Technology is just a base on which to build a personal creative journey, often in countertendency. You have to learn the technique to conquer it, to innovate, even through errors (involuntary or calculated) that enable artists – accustomed to using technology without becoming slaves to it – to create a style. The risk otherwise is always the same: to repeat the same things done by others, applying the technique in a standardised way and therefore without personality. Art is made by artists, not by computers.

Software is a fundamental tool, but without any knowledge of the history of images, without a general cultural background, without research and thought, it becomes an empty exercise, a pastime along the lines of a playstation.

Bruno Di Marino

Researcher of moving images

Introduction

Augmented reality in public spaces

This manual is aimed at enthusiasts and experimenters in the visual field who wish to acquire the skills for creating video mapping performances. It has been done intentionally to enter into the category of texts dealing with Augmented Reality, in that it reflects its principles and objectives.

To date this book is the first text that collects in an organic and comprehensive way all the necessary steps so that the reader, even if inexperienced, can approach video mapping. The topics have, in fact, been dealt with in the light of the increasing difficulty in using the various types of software.

The web offers the chance to see many tutorials on the subject, but none of them explain comprehensively how to achieve a performance: from the choice of location to the survey, from the choice of the projector up to the techniques to capture architecture.

There is currently no single software that allows the complete management of a performance of video mapping, as this discipline encompasses very different skills ranging from sound design to the generation of video clips, through to 3D modeling. Multimedia planning is characterised by cross-disciplinary skills that the contemporary performer must necessarily possess; he must be able to manage different disciplines and software which is increasingly complex and powerful.

Video mapping, with the ability to use open source software, has had a strong initial push that has allowed its progress and dissemination. It can be used in any context in which you want to transform an object into a dynamic display.

In this volume all the topics covered in the various workshops that the gloWArp studio has held on the subject are addressed in a gradual and complete way, providing advice and guidance on practical problems encountered in the course of the professional activity. The experience gained during the application of such techniques in situations of all kinds, from the simplest to the most complex, such as archaeological excavations or organic systems, is the strong point of the book which intends to provide a solid methodological basis for addressing both simple systems described here and more complex systems, which will be developed in Volume 2.

Therefore it represents a teaching aid that allows everyone to learn the technique of video mapping, using it and enhancing it, and later, creating an interactive and comprehensive performance through the use of kinect® or software nodes. The decision to apply the theoretical tools on a real structure which is readily available, allows you to immediately apply the knowledge you have gained and test your level of preparedness for more complex architectural mapping.

Finally, a lot of attention has been paid to the selection of software, in such a way that all readers that intend to approach video mapping – whether they are PC or Mac users – can find in this volume the right training guide for this discipline.

Organisation of the volume

Before entering the world of video mapping we believe it is appropriate to present a simple overview that clarifies the organisational logic of the book and its chapters. The index has in fact been designed so that the reader can delve into the topic and understand the various steps that will lead him to have a basic knowledge of the techniques of video mapping.

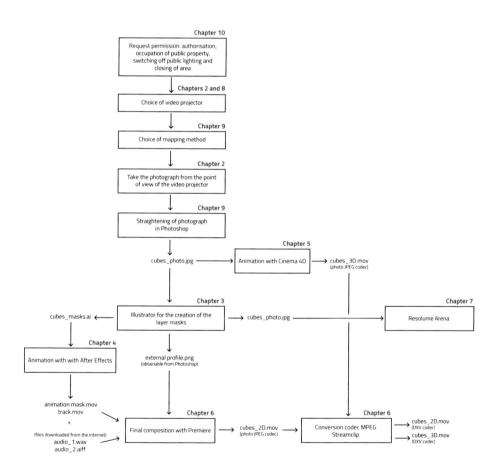

Chapter 1

A brief history of Video Mapping

Architecture is the masterly, correct and magnificent play
of masses brought together in light.

Le Corbusier

Statu Variabilis,
Video mapping performance off
contest, GLOWFestival 2nd
edition, Church of S. Vito Martire,
Ostuni (BR), 2014

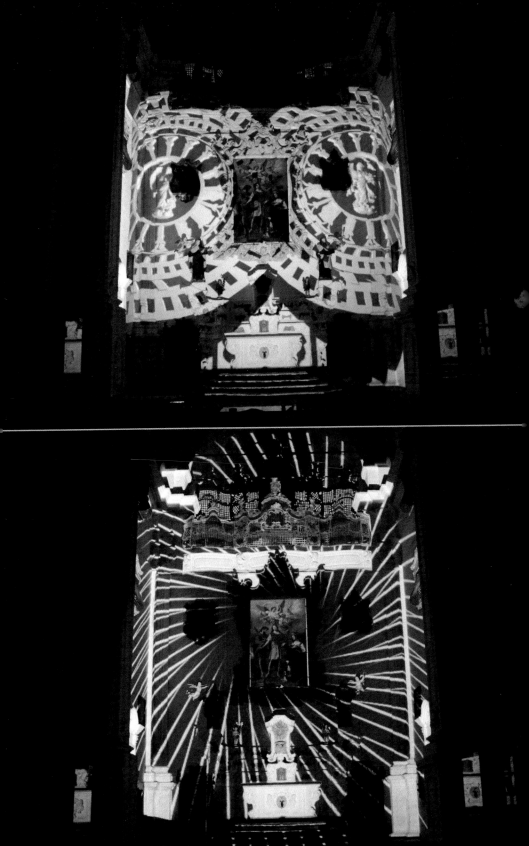

CHAPTER 1

1.1 What is video mapping?

Video mapping (also called 3D mapping, projection mapping, or simply mapping) is a particular form of Augmented Reality (AR), or reality created by the developer, a kind of development of the discipline characterised by greater completeness and consistency.

The term "mapping" has been used since the origins of video mapping to give it a particular connotation which, however, turns out to be purely technical and somewhat simplistic.

Lately, though, when talking about video mapping, in addition to Augmented Reality we refer to "Architectural Dressing", a new term that can attribute to the discipline different connotations and a much deeper meaning[1], to some extent ethical, the result of time and of determining the effects produced by such practice.

Returning to augmented reality, we can say that it consists of enriching, with the mediation and use of a computer, the human sensory perception with the addition of more information than that perceived by the observer. The reality can be "enhanced" through various devices such as a smart phone, webcam, sensor, earphone or in our case through the use of a video projection system. Of course, augmented reality can also remove perceived information, and doing this generates a reality which is clearer or more fun.

---

1. One of these extensions of content is given by Pasquale Direse who in his contribution published in the book "Artificial Light and Cityscape", edited by Vittorio Fiore and Luca Ruzza (published by Lettera Ventidue, 2013) considers "Architectural Dressing like a performing flow that interprets the architecture and public space as a theatre of emerging media. [...] instead of the techno-scientific race towards the smart city and the "global city", it is preferable to proceed in the direction of an intelligent territory which is recognizable and distinguishable. [...] The theatrical space becomes a relational scene of the city as a place to rediscover and reinvent through the use of new media of communication [...]."
According to this definition the urban fabric becomes a media and communicative storyline in which Architectural Dressing demonstrates a crossing of media between the theatre and emerging digital technologies.

Unlike what happens in virtual reality (VR), where the information added or subtracted electronically is prevalent, in augmented reality the viewer continues to perceive and interact with physical reality acquiring additional information.

Augmented reality and virtual reality are not necessarily anti-ethical: to understand the idea we can consider mediated reality as a boundary line with respect to which the designer chooses the type of final development that seems more suitable to him.

Carrying out video mapping uses three geometric transformations – homothety, homography and anamorphism – that correspond to the phases of work and allow for the matching of the virtual model to the real one.

Homothety is a particular geometric transformation of the plane or space that expands or contracts objects, while maintaining the corners, that is to say the shape.

Homography is the relationship between points of two spaces such that each point of space corresponds to one and only one point of the second space.

Anamorphism, however, is a transformation that creates an optical illusion effect for which an image is projected on the surface in a distorted way, making the original subject recognizable only by looking at the picture from a precise location. Examples of anamorphism are the advertising signs drawn on the playing fields of various sports. These are deliberately drawn on the soil in a distorted manner, so that they appear perfectly straight from the point of view of the cameras filming the sports event. The technique has been known for centuries and was used by many artists. One notable example is the painting "The Ambassadors" (figure I.1) of 1533 by Hans Holbein the Younger. In this painting you can see a figure below which is not easy to decipher. To understand it, you have to twist the vision of the image until you realise that the figure in question (the object at the base of the two subjects) is a skull.

Another example of anamorphism is the fresco on the ceiling of the Church of Sant'Ignazio di Loyola in Campo Marzio in Rome (1685) by Andrea Pozzo (figure I.2), in which the virtuosity of the artist allows him to arrange the bodies on three-dimensional surfaces, deforming them to the point that only when looked at from a specific point of view, they appear to be correct.

This technique has been echoed by contemporary artists who have realised the great potential of communication. One example is the Englishman Julian Beever (figures I.3 and I.4), who specialises in painting anamorphic works on pavements in such a way that passers-by perceive cavities or three-dimensional objects that do not really exist.

Figure I.1 – The Ambassadors, Hans Holbein the Younger, 1533.

Figure I.2 – Fresco in the church of Sant'Ignazio di Loyola in Campo Marzio, Roma, Andrea Pozzo, 1685.

Another example is the Swiss Felice Varini (figures I.5 and I.6) that uses the city itself (buildings, courtyards, porticoes) to give touches of high virtuosity to the technique of anamorphism. However, the characteristic constant in each of these works is that the result of what they produce is visible from a single point of view.

Figure I.3 – Pavement drawing, Anamorphic illusions di Julian Beever.

Figure I.4 – Pavement drawing, Anamorphic illusions di Julian Beever.

Figure I.5 – Eight Rectangles, Felice Varini, 2007.

Figure I.6 – Between full and empty, Felice Varini, 2003.

We can certainly affirm that video mapping started with the advent of cinema and that it can now consider itself a particular case of mapping: projection on a flat surface. If we look to the past it is possible to find interesting traces of early experiments in which projections and video projections were used; such experiments have laid the foundations for video installation as they are conceived today. Representative of this is the example "Direct Projections" by Bruno Munari (figures I.7 and I.8), who in the 50's produced this series of visual experiments, differentiating them in to static and dynamic.

Real works of art produced using a mixed technique, which he himself defined as "frescoes of light", they were made by inserting some material between two glass slides which were later projected onto surfaces with a single wide-angle projector. Munari is a great experimenter and through his installations he was one of the first to "draw with light". These installations can be considered, in some respects, the forerunners of a practice that a few decades later would see the projections as protagonists in the contemporary art scene. Munari, in fact, did experiments from which he obtained, by simple rotations and exploiting the particulate nature of light, interesting motion effects. His is the insight of being able to transform light into space, and to him is due the distinction of having used the same light as the medium of painting. An interesting observation is found in Domus n. 291 of 1954 of which this is an excerpt:

MUNARI'S DIRECT PROJECTIONS

Munari has recently projected hundreds of compositions, in large format, in Milan – here we see some of them – made with light; with various materials - transparent, translucent and opaque, violently coloured or with very delicate colours; with plastic materials cut, torn, burned, scratched, melted, engraved, ground; with plant and animal tissues; with artificial fibres, chemical solutions, and (as is stated on the invitation to the projections) with the help of his son Alberto. The artist's work is the same as using oil paint, canvas and brushes, only that instead of oil-based paints, plastic transparent coloured materials have been used; instead of the canvas the composition has been projected directly in a large scale on a white wall; and instead of the brush, light has been used. The possibilities of composition and expression are many; the colour can take on all shades from the brightest and most violent, unattainable by other means, to the more subtle and muted. With chemical solutions, changes of plastic materials, physical actions on the same, you can achieve very interesting "pictorial material". You can use textures and films for certain effects, the opaque parts becoming black in projection, and with several layers of coloured cellophane you can obtain the most varied shades of colour. Indeed, there is a wide palette with which you can deal with any aesthetic problem. Modern life has given us music on discs (and no one thinks of calling an orchestra to come to the home in order to listen to music): now it gives us projected paintings; and everyone close to a disco can have his own projected art gallery made, however, of original and numbered copies, to be projected. Overall dimensions of a collection of one hundred "pictures": 5 cm x 5 cm x 30 cm. A collector can easily take them with them when they travel, to project them on the ceiling of his hotel room, when he wants to see them, any size from ten centimetres to ten metres".

Figure I.7 – Direct Projection, Bruno Munari.

Almost simultaneously, in California, another artist added another element to the history of projections: James Turrell. A lover of minimalism and eclecticism, in 1966 Turrell rented an entire disused hotel which became a studio in which to exhibit his own works. In this venue his "Cross Corner Projection" was shown for the first time. Light from an haolgen projector was passed through pierced metal plates, with a precise inclination on the corner formed by two walls, giving the viewer the illusion that there is a suspended solid shape. In this way Turrell transformed light into volume (figures I.9 and I.10). The best known of these projections was the Afrum (later renamed Afrum-Proto).

Figure I.8 – Direct Projection, Bruno Munari.

Figure I.9 – Afrum, James Turrell.

Figure I.10 – Afrum, James Turrell.

In 1967 his first solo exhibition was staged at the Pasadena Art Museum.

The use of the corner has been taken up by Joanie Lemecier of the AntiVJ collective with her installation of video mapping presented at the Mapping Festival in Geneva in 2012 entitled: "Eyjafjallajökull" in which he himself claimed to have taken his inspiration from Turrell's work (figure I.11). Another example is the installation "Onion Skin" by Oliver Ratsi (AntiVJ) (figure I.12).

Returning to the end of the 60's, 1969 to be precise, Disney, always very attentive to innovations, created that which to all effects was considered a real "proto-mapping". The first projection on an uneven surface was at the opening of the Haunted Mansion ride in Disneyland. The installation called "Grim Grinning Ghosts" (figure I.13) consisted of five busts singing, with mirth, a song performed by Buddy Bucker. With a 16 mm camera the faces of real people were taken, projected on busts, creating the illusory effect of singing sculptures. The system was also later used by some contemporary artists who have fixed faces on other media for their visual installations as in the case of the New York artist Tony Oursler, known for the multimedia works that have made him famous. His works are, in fact, often video-projected on spherical surfaces, which enhance the expression of the subject, in the act of talking, shouting or watching. Combining different mediums such as sculpture, multimedia projections and recordings of the human voice, he seeks interaction with the audience in an almost dreamlike space (figure I.14).

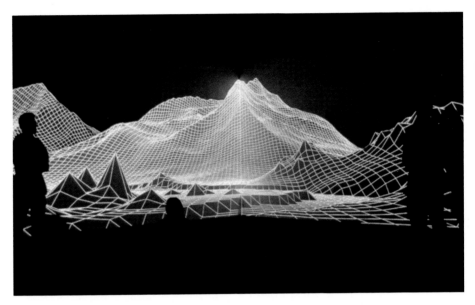

Figure I.11 – Eyjafjallajökull, Joanie Lemecier (AntiVJ), Mapping Festival, 2012.

Figure I.12 – Onion Skin, Oliver Ratsi (AntiVJ).

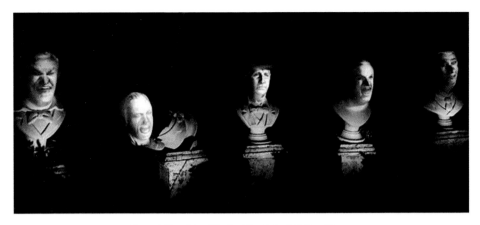

Figure I.13 – Grim Grinning Ghosts installation, Disney.

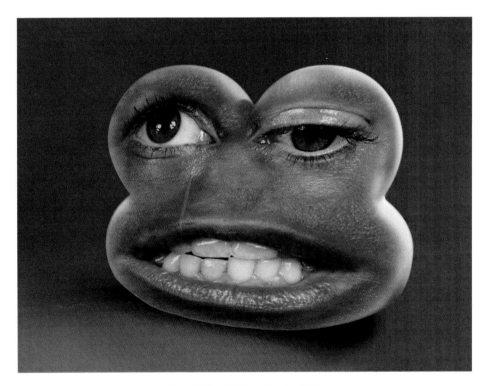

Figure I.14 – XES, Tony Oursler, 2005.

In the 80's experimentation begins to be more interesting and we largely see it divided between indoor experimentation by the American artist Michael Naimark (www.naimark. net), and one of the first documented architectural video projections, by the great Florentine Italian artist Mario Mariotti. Michael Naimark was one of the first experimenters in the field of video mapping and the author of many articles about the more structured beginning of this interesting discipline. His installation "Displacements" (figure I.15), made using analogue technologies, can be considered one of the first examples of "complex mapping".

Figure I.15 – Displacements, Michael Naimark.

Naimark has created an immersive installation reproducing a corner of a living room in an American home. Two actors were shot with a 16mm camera that rotated while they were interacting in the scene. Subsequently the scene was completely painted white and the videos were projected on this: the scene coincided perfectly, except for the people who seemed a bit unreal. In 1984, "Displacements" was reproduced for the third time in San Francisco at the Museum of Modern Art. After twenty years, in 2005, a new edition using digital techniques was proposed, filming the same actors who had taken part in the first production.

Subsequently, as often happens, such installations have been the inspiration for others who have perfected the technique using newly found tools in the digital field. This is the case with Sony which created, with a masterful use of anamorphic techniques, the "Sony Real Time Projection Mapping", whose video went around the world in just a few hours in 2011 (figures I.16 and I.17) .

Figure I.16 – Sony Real Time Projection Mapping, Sony.

Figure I.17 – Sony Real Time Projection Mapping, Sony.

Still in the 80's, in Italy, the Florentine Mario Mariotti, already famous for having created pictures on hands called "Animani", which produced with irony and talent various types of animals, showed some projections on the facade of the church of Santo Spirito in Florence, left unfinished by Brunelleschi, on which he invited famous artists, friends and students to complete them by drawing, according to their own imagination, the contents within the silhouette which was provided (figure I.18).

Figure I.18 – Reconstruction of the projection on the facade of the church of Santo Spirito in Florence, Mario Mariotti.

What leaves you amazed is seeing how the effects produced by the artist imitate in full many of those which we are used to seeing in a contemporary video mapping performance, bringing forward almost thirty years of research in the field of video that today we almost take for granted.

In 1994 Disney, as already seen a forerunner in the field of mapping, registered the first patent that exploited this technique. The name is "Apparatus and method for projection upon a three-dimensional object" and largely sets out the technique of digital painting on real three-dimensional objects. The patent, which is downloadable from the internet[2], features a document that highlights how this technique had raised a lot of interest among researchers (figure I.19).

2. http://www.google.com/patents/US5325473

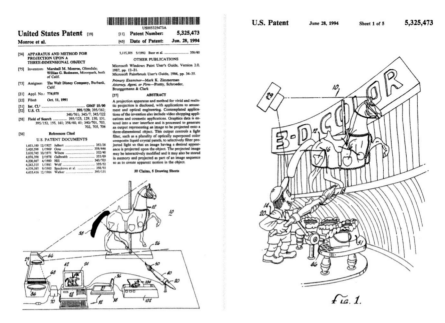

Figure I.19 – Apparatus and method for projection upon a three-dimensional object, Disney, 1994.

From reading the text of the filed patent you can sense the scope of the invention: the processing device included a computer with graphics software and a monitor attached. In particular, some specific software had been designed to store the data of the graphics produced and save them in a memory so as to retrieve them for later projection. An alternative method for projecting an image was also provided. The method included the steps of inserting graphic data in the graphic input device and processing the data to generate an output that would show an image corresponding to the shape of the object's surface. The filter light, subsequently, was controlled in response to the output to filter light from the projector so that the image was projected on the object according to the desired appearance. The output could be stored in a buffer and then developed by the user to interactively modify the image. In addition, the output, which shows the image, could be stored in the memory for later recall and projection on the object. In this regard, a plurality of outputs could also be stored to form a sequence of images which were different, but related, so as to have a sequential projection and simulate idea of motion. Video mapping as we know it today started in 2001, thanks to the work of five researchers from the MIT[3] who published a scientific article entitled "Shader Lamps: Animating Real Objects With Image-Based Illumination". It is amazing to see the breadth of applications

---

3. http://web.media.mit.edu/~raskar/Shaderlamps/

that their research involves, in fields that we now take for granted. One thing that strikes you is seeing the scale model of the Taj Mahal mausoleum in India (figure I.20) used as an example to project and test shadows and effects, and to see that some twelve years after the same technique was used on another large full-scale monument, it formally recalls the previous: the Grand Mosque in Abu Dhabi by Obscura Digital (figure I.21).

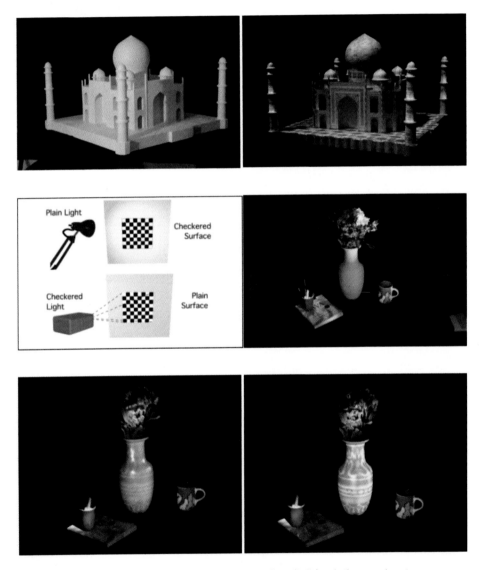

Figure I.20 – Scale model of the Taj Mahal mausoleum (India) and other experiments.

Figure I.21 – Projection on the Grande Moschea in Abu Dhabi by Obscura Digital.

Focussing attention on Italy for a moment, we can state that it has been, and continues to be, a nation in which research and experimentation have made an enormous contribution to the advancement of video mapping.

The first projection associated with architecture is iconic, created by Claudio Sinatti[4] in 2005, with the title "Today's the day the teddy bears have their picnic" (figure I.22). It represented the reconstruction of an underwater landscape populated by bears and squirrels (defined by the author as a "video trompe l'oeil") outside which there was a flight of stairs (real) from which the animals descended or poked out from the bushes, chasing each other up the tree trunks. The sound design was very interesting and well thought out, thanks to the specific placing of the speakers at the points where the animals appeared, giving a faithful and realistic reproduction of sounds.

Equally significant is the interactive installation of indoor video mapping presented by Sinatti in Turin at the PalaFuksas, in 2007 (figure I.23). Sinatti, using Isadora®[5] software, created a custom interface with which he could manage the complexity of the projections. On the ground floor of the structure he placed three video projectors which mapped

4. Well-known artist and designer, who recently died, a pioneer of research in the field of motion art and generative art.

5. Isadora is a graphic programming environment, enhanced by Mark Coniglio in collaboration with the choreographer Dawn Stoppiello, that allows the manipulation of digital videos in real time through controlled impulses of movement.

a large number of connected surfaces, giving the illusion of a much larger number of sources; the images were video loops made interactive through the audio.

Figure I.22 – Today's the day the teddy bears have their picnic, Claudio Sinatti, 2005.

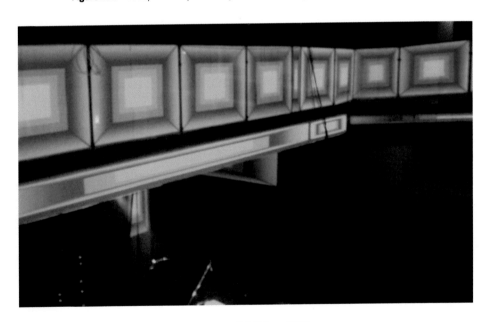

Figure I.23 – PalaFuksas, 2007.

Almost contemporaneous to the research by Sinatti is that carried out by the OpenLab Company[6], which created the installation "Magic Lucigrafie" in 2006 for the "Notte

---

6. Company founded in 1991 in Rome by the performer Laura Colombo and the architect and scenographer Luca Ruzza.

Bianca" (all-night festival) in Rome (figure I.24). Staged at Villa Torlonia, it is one of the first installations of video mapping in which images, sounds and words in motion create an enchanting atmosphere with a strong emotional impact. This performance is only one of many that over the years of the OpenLab Company's activity has encompassed work on several fronts of multimedia design, especially in the field of interactivity within the performance and theatrical setting. The research carried out by the OpenLab Company has made a substantial contribution to the training of students and researches interested in technical and performance aspects in the field of visual arts.

Figure I.24 – Magiche Lucigrafie, Notte Bianca, Roma, Villa Torniola, OpenLab Company, 2006.

It can be claimed that to date Italy is, internationally, among the most thriving countries as regards research in the field of visual and performance culture, and in particular in video mapping, thanks to the contribution of collectives such as Studio Azzurro[7].
An interesting example of the production of Studio Azzurro is the installation "Risveglio" of 2011 in the Piazza della Scala at Milano (figure I.25).

---

7. In the biography of Studio Azzurro, found on the website www.studioazzurro.com, is written: "the artistic research, at the beginning, was directed at achieving a video environment, in which the integration of electronic images and physical environment can be experimented, with the intention of making the spectator central in the perceptual path in which he is involved. The video environments are narrative machines based on a highly descriptive scene, on video recorded sequences of reiterated small events and a monitor composition, that encourages the dissolution of the screen's limits".

Figure I.25 – Risveglio, Studio Azzurro, 2011.

The numerous festivals, completely dedicated to multimedia disciplines and especially video mapping and light as an artistic medium, held even in Italy, should also be mentioned. These festivals, begun in the wake of Architectural Dressing – according to which technology plays a key role as a an aggregator, a "totem", around which "creative tribes reinvent architecture and design intangible urban scenography" – clearly represent great national and international interest in the digital arts. Examples are: the Kernel Festival in Monza (www.kernelfestival.net), the LPM in Rome (www.liveperformersmeeting.net), the Flussi Festival in Avellino (www.flussi.eu), and the GLOWFestival in Ostuni (www .glowfestival.it). To conclude this brief overview of the origins of video mapping and its evolution, two artists should be mentioned, Pablo Valbuena and Joanie Lemecier, who almost contemporaneously have brought video mapping to the highest levels of form and technical complexity.

In particular in 2007 the French artist Pablo Valbuena (figure I.26) began a series of works entitled "Augmented sculptures" which introduce to mapping some new elements: the possibility of doing it indoors, and so not only on large buildings, and of using it as an artistic medium.

In 2013, in his latest works, entitled "Time tilings", video projection goes beyond ordinariness and is spread on completely ordinary surfaces such as public paving.

"I node"[8], onthe other hand, is one of the first works by Joanie Lemecier (AntiVJ[9]) who in 2007 presented a video on YouTube whose description is Live "paper folding" and synchronized mapping on Electronica music. The novelty lies in having introduced to this discipline some elements that have then characterised it, becoming a reference point for many, beyond that of inspiration, such as the use of minimalism in the effects, made unique by the absolute simplicity of the form of the projections and the use of electronic music, equally minimalist, which ties in well with their projections.

The continuing and increasing interest in this discipline is represented by the permanent outdoor installations of video mapping like Breda Castel Hungary created by László Zsolt Bordos in Hungary and Omicron by the AntiVJ collective, Poland.

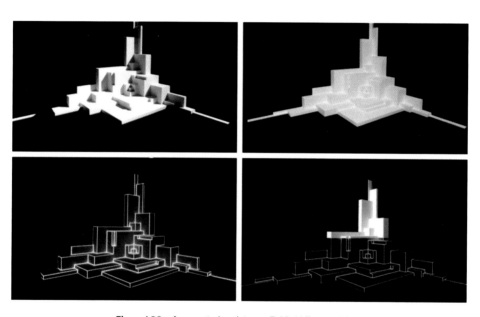

Figure I.26 – Augmented sculptures, Pablo Valbuena, 2007.

---

8. http://www.youtube.com/watch?v=_9y1Tesw4YY

9. http://www.antivj.com – AntiVJ is a Visual Lab created by five European artists who, over the years, have paved the way to an increasingly refined visual, as well as collaborations with artists in the musical field, realising the great communicative potential that music and video can transmit. Their work is focussed on the use of light, its perception and the performance produced by it, moving away from standard techniques and configurations, to offer unique experiences in the search for both form and experimentation. They were the forerunners of the use of open source software, with and without nodes, for creating customised interfaces, and have created real customised programs, in some cases shared with people on the web: it is the philosophy of DIY (Do it Yourself) and DIT (Do it Together). With their research they have introduced the characterstic of artistry and uniqueness that makes their accomplishments real art installations. In 2008, one of their first performances, in Brussels during an all-night festival, lays the foundation of the great adventure of video mapping in its current meaning.

1.2 What is the future for video mapping?

The future of video mapping coincides with the technical possibilities offered by the evolution of programming. At a time when it has become a technique of infinite expressive potential, many collectives have used it for events, festivals and exhibitions. To talk about the future is a delicate operation because of the speed with which technological processes advance, meaning it is not able to consolidate what has already been produced. It is evident how its use has soon involved different fields.

Originally used only for artistic experimentation, video mapping is now used in more commercial sectors such as advertising big brands that want to publicise the launch of innovative products.

The increasing possibilities offered by pure experimentation, thanks to the spiraling calculating power of computers and access to increasingly simple information (eg. tutorials), have allowed the experimentation of interactive forms complementary to video mapping. We are witnessing events in which the audience itself becomes part of the event through interaction by means of sensors, infrared cameras or stereoscopic cameras such as Kinect®. Such research is the result of a digital culture devoted to experimentation and created thanks to the contribution of artists such as Nam June Paik, the founding father of video art. His research on the distortion of television images and his works seem to have foreseen the use of video for such purposes, especially in cases where assembling old televisions and distorting the video made them resemble great displays. An example is the installation Electronic Superighway (figure I.27).

Likewise, it is worth mentioning the contribution of artists such as Richard Barbrook and Pit Schultz who in 1997 wrote and disseminated "The Digital Artisans Manifesto" through the Internet, which in twenty-four articles claimed the importance of digital creativity in building the society of tomorrow, coining a term until then unknown: the digital artisan. "We are digital artisans. We celebrate the Promethean energy of our work and our imagination to give shape to the virtual world. By hacking, writing code, designing and mixing, we build the interconnected future thanks to our commitment and our creativity "[10].

The future of this practice is intimately connected to its history: the future is to experiment, but it will also be in its content. Although today most video mapping is counted only in the category of visual shows, there are artists that transpose these effects brilliantly , both audio and video, in its own research that verges in some cases on the canons of their video art.

---

10. Translation of the first article of *The Digital Artisans Manifesto*.

Figure I.27 – Electronic Superhighway, Nam June Paik.

1.3 Vjing and video mapping: what are the differences?

A VJ o vee-jay (video jockey) is an artist-performer who mixes, projects or organises in a live performance, a show of lights and and visual effects using clips of videos, slides, lights, lasers or anything else, that goes in time to music (usually the accompanying music is electronic). The VJ in this capacity can also create video installations, or be a performer detached from the activity of entertainment. From VJ has arisen the expression VJing, which is the art of mixing video streams strengthened by music. Fifteen years ago this artistic expression was still unknown but it appears to have begun in the techno scene of the 90's. The expression was made famous by the American TV channel MTV as it originally referred to the presenters of music video clips[11]. Over time, the concept of the VJ has evolved and has been increasingly associated with the creators of video content which they distorted or mixed in real time. The role of VJ has evolved both from the point of view of technique and from what concerns the styles of music associated with it: initially only minimal music and electronics, later also jazz and classical music. The VJ

---

11. Definition of VJ given by wikipedia.

culture[12] has quickly spread and united electronic music and visual art mainly from the club culture.

When technical possibilities have allowed, the VJs have come out in the open "invading" public spaces and in many cases distinguishing their performances.

Based on what has been said, it is possible to consider video mapping as a branch of VJing and this explains why, in making video mapping performances, software dedicated to Vjing is usually used.

But what are the differences between these two disciplines? In reality video mapping being a branch of Vjing, the differences should be minimal or none but, if you analyse the way in which each of them is designed, very substantial differences are also noticed. Differences of no small importance are the concept (storyboard) that gives form to an event of video mapping and its related content that generally "should" be less random and more meaningful than the contents of a Vjing performance.

Usually in a Vjing event there is no preparation of layer masks (see chapter 3); in the classic version you project on a screen or on a completely flat surface, but for some years the practice has evolved and more complex and articulated performance surfaces are used that can be mapped, adding a higher quality value to the final show, the so called "stage mapping" (figure I.28). Stage mapping consists of projecting video content on physical installations with a structure formed by tetrahedrons, cubes and triangular surfaces, which in some cases imitate the installations of the artist Martin Böttger (figure I.29) or the works of the visionary architect Lebbeus Woods (figure I.30).

Figure I.28 – Example of stage mapping.

---

12. For more information, we advise reading the book Vj Audio-Visual Art + vj culture, by Michael Faulkner edited by Laurence King Publishing, 2006.

Figure I.29 – Splitter, Martin Böttger.

Figure I.30 - SCAR construction, Lebbeus Woods, Sarajevo.

Even contemporary artists in the musical field have understood the importance of putting the video to music: a typical case is that of Alva Noto (figure I.31) who with the performance Unidisplay, at the Hangar Bicocca in Milan, links electronic music to minimal visuals; equally significant is the latest performance of Plastikman at the Guggenheim Museum in New York (figure I.32), or the collaboration between Ryuichi Sakamoto and Alva Noto in which piano and electronic music converge into a single project entitled Summvs (figure I.33), which evokes many associations and combines the Latin words "sum" and "versus", summarizing the creative process that takes place between the two artists in which music and visual effects converge in a holistic work.

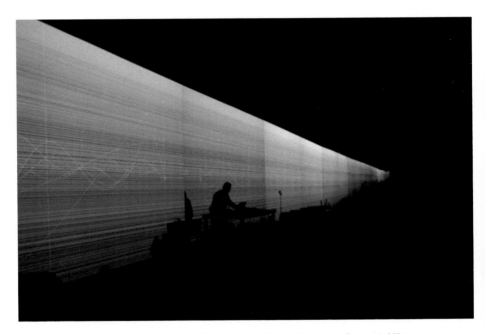

Figure I.31 – Performance Unidisplay by Alva Noto at the Hangar Bicocca in Milano.

Returning to video mapping, you can see that its most complex phase is the preparation of the mapping files that represent the basic building blocks for the creation of any video content. From these files, which will form the basis for creating 2D and/or 3D content, you can build a story according to a concept and create the final video in post-production just like any other video. There is a hybrid mode between VJing and video mapping that takes advantage of the creation of layer masks by varying the video content on the pierced parts of the "alpha channel" creating a "false mapping". To create mapping in real time means that the performer is always active on the work console. This requires good technical training in order to manage the effects and sequences with a controller, an operation whose success can only be guaranteed by experience and time. Usually, if the work must be completed in a short time, for which it is not possible to create all that complex sequence and studied content, a solution that can be us

With false mapping, once the mapping of the facade is created, yc

of as many layer masks as there are effects that you want to inte

channel allows the general video to appear only in the desired parts

that for certain elements, rather than others, you have created an ad not video. its name

derives from the fact that, through the use of layer masks the complexity of the facade in its entirety is not taken into account but only the elements that are appropriate to display the video concerned. The experience is very useful in the evaluation phase of the final effects because everything you see on screen is unlikely to be an exact representation of what you will see once the video is shown. What you will project, from colours to shades, will be added to the colours and shadows of any real surface creating, at times, different effects from those intended. A solution to this problem consists in carrying out, if possible, a field test, in order to evaluate what are the sequences to keep and which ones to discard. In video mapping, unlike Vjing in which the videos are usually secondary to the music, video and audio have the same importance. This aspect is often overlooked in performances when in fact it determines the success or otherwise of an event.

Figure I.32 – Plastikman at the Guggenheim Museum, New York.

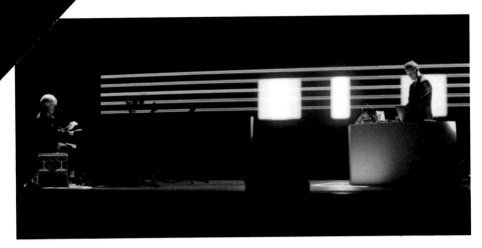

Figure I.33 – Performance Summvs, Ryuichi Sakamoto and Alva Noto.

Doing video mapping means moving people and producing whatever is necessary to captivate both the ears and the eyes. When video mapping is available to all and represents the new "contemporary fireworks" the difference will be just in the content.

1.4 Brief overview of existing software and that used in this volume

From the beginnings of video mapping until today, computers have become increasingly powerful, and various types of software have been produced, open source and otherwise, dedicated to that purpose. The controls for carrying out video mapping have very often been often included in the software for VJs but over time it has been noticed that the video mapping requires specific controls as well as particular attention to the set up. For this reason, while some Vjing software have included modules and filters for video distortion within them (usually the term used is "warping"), in the meantime software dedicated specifically to video mapping has been produced.

The difference in the operating system (Mac or PC) has further divided end users. It is not uncommon to find software that has everything that meets our needs on Mac but not on PC or vice versa.

The trend in recent years, in real time generation of content, has brought further innovations in the field of audio-video production, as it has gone from programming with languages like Processing®, which requires knowledge of Java, to the production of content based nodes, creating what in the jargon are called "patches". This new way of designing has greatly simplified traditional programming in that, being composed of modules, usually pre-set, users can use them like parts of an engine that allows them to assembly their own performance.

Among the most important node software are: Quartz composer®, Touch Designer® Pure Data®, VVVV®. Some of these interact very well with the most common VJing programs such as Resolume® and Modul8®, for which you can create special controls and customise any part according to the demands of the performance.

The software to be used for the screening of content is not a major issue, because it will serve mainly to make additional "adjustments" on the final video (the aforementioned "warping") to match the video to the structure for which it was intended.

One senses that it is not essential to use VJing software for mapping but a program would suffice which could distort the four vertices and divide the video into a mesh, so as to allow the global and local distortion according to the two axes x and y. In this regard we have provided a list of suitable open source software and the links from which to download them:

- **warpmap®** - Mac and PC

  http://www.playmodes.com/index.php?option=com_content&view=article&id=118:warpmap-first-release-&catid=41:researchgeneral

- **meshwarp®** - Mac and PC

  http://meshwarpserver.org/?page_id=10

- **VPT®** - Mac and PC (the first warping software)

  http://hcgilje.wordpress.com/vpt/

- **Lpmt®** - Mac, PC and Linux

  http://hv-a.com/lpmt/

If instead you want some software developed exclusively for VJing with warping modules for video mapping, there is:

- **Resolume Arena®** o **Avenue** – Mac and PC
- **Modul8®** - Mac
- **vdmx®** - Mac
- **Arkaos®** - Mac e PC
- **flxer®** - open source Mac, PC and Linux

Among the best programs developed ad hoc for video mapping there are:

- **Millumin®** - Mac
- **Mad mapper®** - Mac

Finally we list some node (patch) programs, open source and others, with which you can also use for warping:

- **Quartz composer®** - Mac
- **Pure data®** - Mac e PC
- **Isadora®** - Mac e PC
- **VVVV®** - PC
- **Touch designer®** - PC

The software referred to represents the best offered by the market (open source and others) and for which more information is available on the internet.

1.5 Compression formats and codecs

This section is a kind of small glossary of some terms that are used in parts of this volume where saving videos in various formats and their use in video mapping software is discussed.

Interlacing

Often while saving in programs like Adobe Premiere® or Mpeg Streamclip®, there is an option about interlacing. We talk about interlacing in TV and this is when the lines making up the image are drawn alternating equal lines with odd. 576 lines are sent in two phases 288 equal + 288 equal odd. In contrast to the interlacing mode, the progressive mode is when the image is drawn in a single step, i.e. 576 lines simultaneously. You should be aware of this mode as misuse can affect the quality of the video. Saving a video in interlaced mode, and not progressive, means that while playing the video you will see unsightly horizontal lines, especially during movement.

Frame Rate

The Frame Rate is the number of frames transmitted per second and it is expressed in FPS; the higher the frame rate, the greater the fluidity of the video. The standard frame rate is 25fps and, since being introduced in Europe in the early 60s, it is the reference point for most Western European countries.

Bit-Rate

The bit-rate is measured in bits/s (bits per second) and indicates the number of bits used to define an image, essentially determining its quality. With a bit-rate of 4000 Kbit/sec it is possible to define a frame well; with only 300 Kbit/sec, quality decays considerably. There is no "best bit-rate" for a compressed video, but there is a bit-rate which is necessary to meet the specific requirements related to the characteristics of the video. In cases where a low resolution is used, it is possible to set the value of the bit-rate higher. By setting a bit-rate which is too high you are likely to create a "heavy" file which plays with typical jerky display problems and loss of synchronism. Two types of bit-rate can be used: VBR (Variable Bit Rate) or CBR (Constant Bit Rate). The VBR is the most widely used type, and has a variable bit-rate from a minimum value to a maximum value: the higher the value of the bit-rate, the greater will be the definition of the scene. Instead, the CBR parameter has a fixed value bit-rate and forces the frame to use only that specific value, even if the scene could use a lower bit-rate. This results in a smaller compression file than when the VBR parameter is used, which represents the best choice in case of limited space without sacrificing quality.

Compression Codecs

Codec stands for encoder-decoder and indicates the use of a particular algorithm that allows you to record, transmit and store the video. Understanding the best compression to be used in each specific case is essential because it allows you to create videos that are then decoded by the software used to project and make video mapping. The use of the optimal codec helps the video, even if of excellent quality, avoid going jerky or even stopping. Every manufacturer of mapping software has its own compression codec.

If you do not use compression, even a few minutes of video could take up many gigabytes. Making, for example, reference to a 10-minute video in XGA (1024 x 768 px), with a value equal to 25 FPS, and assuming that each picture uses 100 Kbytes, the final video would amount to 1.5 Gbytes (25 FPS x 60 sec x 10 min x 100 Kbytes = 1500000 Kbytes = 1.5 Gbytes). From this simple example the need to use codecs that allow you to optimise the space taken up by video is clear. Choosing the right codec and setting the parameters correctly will make the difference between a good export of the video or not.

There are two types of compression: **intra-frame compression** and **inter-frame compression**.

In the **intra-frame compression** individual frames are compressed to further reduce the size of the video. Examples of codecs that use intra-frame compression are JPEG Motion and JPEG Photo codecs in which the images are coded or compressed as individual JPEG images. In JPEG Motion format, for example, the three images in the sequence shown in figure I.34 are coded and sent as separate unique images with no links between them and they are compressed as individual JPEG images.

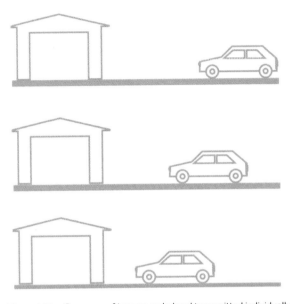

Figure I.34 – Sequence of images coded and transmitted individually.

The **inter-frame compression**, however, is a compression in which the frames vary continuously. Only the first frame is stored completely while for the subsequent frames only the differences with the first are stored. Examples are the algorithms of video compression, MPEG-4 and H.264, that use compression to reduce video data between a series of frames. This involves techniques such as differential coding, where each frame is compared with that of the reference frame and only the pixels modified with respect to the reference frame are encoded. Therefore, the number of pixel values coded and sent is significantly reduced (figure I.35). When viewing a sequence encoded in this way, the images are reproduced as in the original video sequence.

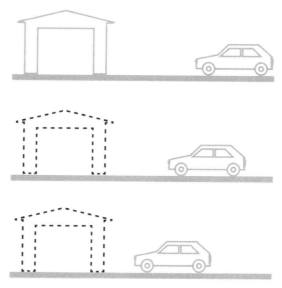

— Trasmitted - - Not trasmitted

Figure I.35 – Sequence of images with differential coding.

To further reduce the data and so the size of the video, you can use other techniques such as block-based motion compensation. This technique identifies the part of a new frame in a video sequence which corresponds to that of a previous frame, even if it is in a different position, and divides the frame into a series of macroblocks (blocks of pixels). This allows you to create or "anticipate", block after block, a new frame, looking for a block which matches in the reference frame. If a match is found, the encoder codes the position where the corresponding block in the reference frame is found.

The more advanced the compression algorithm, the higher the latency. Latency is the time it takes to compress, send, decompress and display a file.

Generally, the **video codec** based on different standards are incompatible with each other, which means that a compressed video according to a certain standard cannot be decompressed with a different standard. The following describes the most common compression formats that can be chosen in video software mapping and VJing as an option when exporting in various programs such as After Effects®, Cinema 4D® or Premiere®.

Photo JPEG

The Photo JPEG codec is implemented by the Joint Photographic Experts Group (JPEG ISO version 9R9), an algorithm for image compression. It is generally used to store high-quality video.

In QuickTime format, there are three JPEG codecs: Photo JPEG, MJPEG-A, and MJPEG-B. The use of this standard involves the production of high-quality video with little compression.

Motion JPEG

Motion JPEG or M-JPEG is a digital video sequence consisting of a series of individual JPEG images. The principle of Motion JPEG (abbreviation M-JPEG or MJPEG, not to be confused with MPEG) is to apply the compression algorithm subsequently to the various images of a video sequence.

Because there are no links between the frames in the Motion JPEG format, if one frame is lost during the transmission, the rest of the video will not be compromised. The main disadvantage in the use of the standard Motion JPEG is the fact that it does not use video compression techniques to reduce the data, as it consists of a series of still, complete images.

MPEG-4

Like all standard MPEGs (Moving Picture Experts Group) MPEG-4 is a codec which can be purchased with a licence. It supports applications with limited bandwidth and applications that require high quality images, without any limits to the transmission speed and with virtually unlimited bandwidth.

H.264

The H.264 standard, also known as the MPEG-4 Part 10 / AVC (AVC stands for Advanced Video Coding), is the latest MPEG standard for video encoding. It is expected to become the most widely used video standard. An encoder that supports the H.264 standard is able to reduce the size of a digital video file by more than 80% compared with the Motion JPEG format and up to 50% compared to standard MPEG-4, without compromising on the quality of images. This means that managing video files will require less storage space and bandwidth, or rather that it is possible to obtain higher quality images at the same transmission speed in bits.

The H.264 standard is likely to accelerate the spread of high-definition video as this ultra-efficient compression technology can reduce the size of the file and the transmission speed in bits without compromising image quality.

DXV Codec (Resolume)

The DXV codec, specially created by Resolume, is a codec based on the decompression of frames produced directly on the video card. The high processing power that current video cards possess allows you to work with resolutions and frame rates which are much higher than those that could be used by using the CPU and RAM.

The DXV Codec is a cross-platform Quicktime codec which can be used on any video application that supports rendering to the Quicktime (.mov) file format. Some applications that support it are: QuickTime Player Pro®, Final Cut Pro 7®, Adobe Premiere®, After Effects®, Sony Vegas®, Maya®.

The DXV is a pre-configured codec (it does not have any settings that allow you to adjust the quality, the data rate, and key-frame), which is fast and extremely easy to use.

Chapter 2

How to choose the video projector

In order for the light to shine so brightly, the darkness must be present.

Francis Bacon

Video mapping
performance,
Church of S.
Gerardo at
Maiella, Calvi
(BN), 2011

CHAPTER 2

2.1 Video projector technology

The choice of the projector is a fundamental aspect for the success of a video mapping event. Each video projector, professional or otherwise, has specific features.

For video mapping you can use any type of projector, but of course the choice depends on the context in which it will be used. If you are working on a building, the home theater projector obviously would not be usable; it should be used in an indoor environment instead.

Usually for mapping you use cinema film projectors with technical features and elevated brightness, but it is important to note that the cost of rental varies according to the functionality. The most widely used video projectors use three different technologies: DLP, LCD and Laser.

DLP Projectors (Digital Light Processing)

DLP projectors are based on the use of an optical microchip DMD (Digital Micromirror Device) covered with micro-mirrors whose number defines the resolution of the projector itself. The micro-mirrors are capable of moving independently, following the dynamics of each pixel of the image, and reflect the light beam coming from the projector lamp after it has passed through a colour wheel that spins at very high speed, making the image visible and coloured to the human eye. The DMD chip in turn emits a beam of light that passes through the lens. This technology is subject to a possible anomaly, the "Rainbow" effect (multicoloured flashes visible at certain distances and during certain eye movements).

Avantages
- Simplicity of installation;
- Reduced dimensions and less complexity compared to LCD projectors;
- Reliability and consistency of performance;
- Quality of vision generally higher than LCD projectors (especially for watching films);
- High contrast ratio with good production of the colour black.

Disadvantages
- Noise caused by cooling fan;
- Less bright than LCD projectors;
- More expensive than LCD projectors;
- Short lamp life;
- Screendoor Effect ("mosquito net effect") less than LCD projectors but still present;
- Rainbow Effect.

LCD Video projectors (Liquid Crystal Diode)

LCD video projectors or liquid crystal diode, have dichroic mirrors through which the light comes from the lamp in three beams corresponding to the three primary colours (red, blue and green), and whose pixels define the resolution of the projector. These single-colour images, once channelled on the three sides of a cube-shaped dichroic prism – whose faces are present in LCD panels – are reassembled in the final complete frame that will be projected onto the screen through the lens.

Advantages
- Simplicty of installation (it does not need a complex calibration but only proper placement and correct focus);
- compact dimensions and weight (making transport easier);
- high efficiency;
- elevated brightness (bright images even in a partially illuminated environment);
- faithful production of colours (especially in the case of presentations and graphic images);
- defined framework and accurate focussing;
- low cost.

Disadvantages
- Low contrast ratio (this factor generates a shallow greyscale and generally affects all of the hues of the image);

- Images may appear cold and engraved;
- Screendoor (at a certain distance from the screen the grid of pixels is visible);
- Possible burning of one or more pixels that causes the presence of one or more "dead" points on the picture projected;
- Shot lamp life and high cost of replacement.

Laser video projectors

Laser projectors use lasers instead of the traditional lamp. The laser emits a white light towards the 3 LCD panel, enabling you to achieve exceptional image quality with high brightness, excellent contrast and outstanding colour stability.

Advantages
- Excellent depth of blacks and therefore higher contrast;
- colour stability;
- high brightness;
- low maintenance cost.

Disadvantages
- High cost (new generation technology).

2.2 Features of video projectors

In this section we briefly describe the main features of each projector: Lumens, ANSI Lumens and Lux; Contrast ratio; Resolution; Aspect ratio; Image Size/Throw ratio; Keystone Correction; Size and weight; Brightness of the projector lens.

Lumen, ANSI Lumen e Lux

The value of the brightness of a video projector, measured in ANSI Lumens, is one of the most important factors. It defines the power of the emission of the light bean that projects the video and therefore the ability to produce vivid and brilliant images even if the environment is not completely dark.

An ANSI Lumen is the equivalent of the visible brightness generated by a candle. Understanding the value of brightness which is necessary for your specific case requires a careful evaluation of several factors, including the size of the environment and the general conditions of ambient light.

The difference between Lumens (Lm) and ANSI Lumens is purely technical: while Lumen means the standard unit of measurement of the light flow, the ANSI Lumen is a method of measuring the lumens emitted by the projector (it is a method established by 'American National Standards Institute - ANSI - that defines the procedures for testing the projector).

Having said that, it is important to understand the difference between Lumen and Lux. The Lumen is the unit of measurement of the light flow and it is the unit of measurement of the total light power radiated from a light source in all directions (figure II.1 case A). The Lux, however, is the unit of measurement of the brightness of a light striking a surface detectable with an tool called a lux meter (figure II.1 case B).

Figure II.1 – A) lumen; B) lux.

Contrast ratio

The contrast ratio is the ratio between the brightness of the white and the brightness of the black and together with the brightness defines the quality of vision produced by a video projector. It is responsible for the depth of blacks (a typical point of criticism of LCD and DLP projectors), shades of grey, and in general all the shades of colours. It is expressed in the form of a numerical ratio (for example, 1000:1) between the maximum and minimum brightness; this is also defined by ANSI. The higher this ratio, the higher will be the quality of the image produced. A greater contrast means better images with more saturated colours as the difference between black and white is greater.

When a video projector has a contrast ratio equal to 1000:1 it means that the brightness of a completely white image is 1000 times greater than the brightness of a completely black image. This occurs because, as it is easy to understand, you cannot get an absolute black as the visible one will still be a black projected from a light source.

Resolution

The resolution of the video projector influences the quality of the images projected. It consists of points called "pixels" which together form what the human eye perceives as a single rectangular image. The most widely resolutions used are those shown figure II.2.

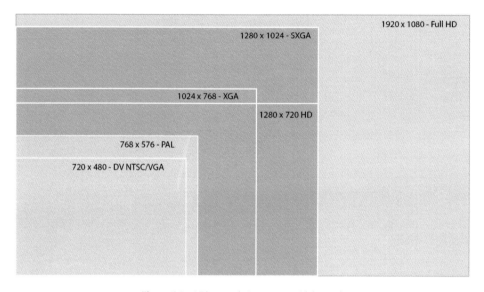

Figure II.2 – Video resolutions most widely used.

The higher the resolution of the video, the better the quality of the image on the screen, provided that the projector reaches that resolution. If you want to project a video with XGA resolution with a SVGA projector, this would result in a loss of definition of the original video, as the device would scale down the video resolution, projecting to a resolution of 800x600. If instead you use an SXGA projector to project a video in XGA resolution, it would be projectable, but in some cases may cause a pixilation or mosaic effect. It is always possible to project a video with a lower resolution than the projector as long as the aspect ratio remains unchanged, so that there are no distortions. Often in the field of video mapping an aspect linked to resolution is underrated: the increase of resolution means better quality video, but this is generally perceived if you view it on a computer monitor. A higher resolution definitely improves the vision of areas of shadow in the rendering (ambient occlusion) or global illumination on monitors, but when the video is projected at a distance (which can also be considerable) and on a large surface, the result of the final vision will be influenced by many factors. The surface may be neither white nor perfectly flat (which will add the effects of the video to those perceived by its projection on the three-dimensional surface) and of no little importance is the position of the viewers who will be at a certain distance from the surface itself. These factors, affecting the appearance of the final vision of the projection, will have an appearance that is sometimes different from the one it had on the monitor.

An especially high resolution could theoretically be advantageous in the process of warping because it would make available more points with which to distort the video, especially when they fall into the sensitive points of the architecture. It goes without saying that a good mapping file needs very few adjustments during warping, and that at times it is counterproductive to greatly increase the mesh as this involves the increase of the points of distortion.

An ideal minimum resolution, based on experience in the field, starts from XGA 1024x768 4:3 format. This resolution has clear advantages: it saves on the cost of the projector, you greatly reduce rendering times, the loss of video quality is very marginal and the aspect ratio, usually, allows the inclusion of most of the facades (in cases where the mapping covers a long, narrow area, it is desirable to interconnect projectors, varying the aspect ratio).

Aspect ratio

Aspect ratio indicates the ratio, i.e. the proportions, between the long and short sides of the video.

Below are the most common aspect ratios and in figure II.3 their correspondence to different video formats.

4:3 Aspect ratio = 1,3 recurring
- 1024x768
- 1152×864
- 1280×960
- 1400×1050

16:9 Aspect ratio = 1,7 recurring
- 1280x720
- 1980x1080

16:10 Aspect ratio = 1,6
- 1440x900
- 1920x1200

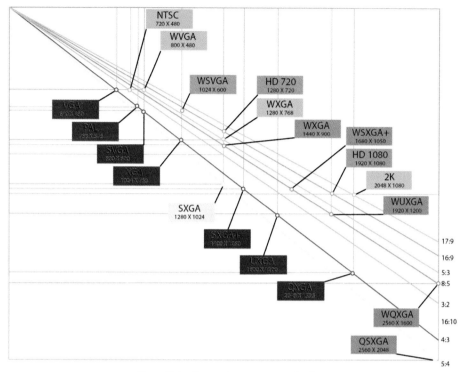

Figure II.3 – The most common aspect ratios.

The aspect ratio, of course, remains constant with distance as the projection is a homothetic type and homothety has among its features that of transforming a geometric figure (in this case the rectangle of the projection) into a similar figure as that given.

Recently film making has witnessed a huge revolution arising with the introduction of digital. The large producers have set new standards for digital cinema projection, defining specifications of 2K and 4K formats, also called Super HD. As shown in figure II.4, Super HD formats (using VP9 as a compression codec) have resulted in a great leap forward compared to Full HD, now widespread even in the home.

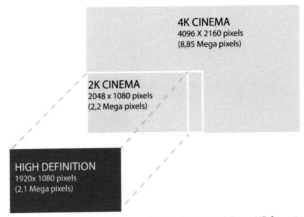

Figure II.4 – Comparison between Full HD format and Super HD formats.

With the same screen, 4K resolution offers a resolution four times greater than Full HD. Technically this resolution means that each frame is the equivalent of a photograph of about 9 Mpixel. For example, if you create a film in 4K at 25fps (25 frames per second), every second of the video has a "weight" of about 130 MB.

Throw ratio (image dimension) = d/b

Throw ratio (TR) is defined as the ratio between the distance from which the projector is placed and the size of the base of the projection surface b (figure II.5). This ratio allows you to calculate the distance required to achieve the desired size.

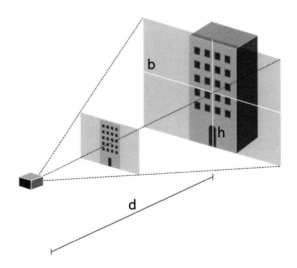

Figure II.5 – Example scheme of Throw ratio.

A TR equal to 1.3-1.8:1 indicates that the projector will project an image with 1 m base, 1.3 m away (with the zoom set to wide-angle) up to 1.8 m away (with telephoto zoom). It is important to know the TR because even with a rough calculation you can obtain the distance at which the projector should be placed. Knowing the right projection distance can be helpful in choosing the projector in terms of weight and portability.

Keystone correction

In cases where the projector is used in a position that is not perpendicular to the plane of projection, the picture projected suffers distortion that deforms the image (instead of a rectangle you have a trapezoid). The keystone correction function allows you to change this distortion.

Size and weight

The size and weight of a video projector are characteristics of no small importance. Both increase with the ANSI lumens, so it is necessary to take them into account as they affect the features of the structure to be used to support it.

Video projector lenses

There are various types of lenses from which to choose the most suitable one according to your needs. They are divided into:

- normal;
- wide-angle;
- telephoto.

The choice depends on the value of the TR which will compared to the values given on the data sheets of the lenses provided by each video projector. Generally a wide angle lens, offering very high performance, is suitable in most situations. In fact, creating a much bigger picture allows you to place the projector at a much shorter distance from the projection surface resulting in less light loss. When particular circumstances force the placement of the projector far from the surface, a telephoto lens will be needed. The practical example shown in the following chapters will remove any doubt.

2.3 Setting a scene type: projecting indoors on cubes

In this volume an exercise that is simple to implement, which uses cardboard cubes arranged in an indoor environment (figure II.6), and a video projector, has been chosen as the main theme for the first steps in video mapping. Practising this "simplified model" is important as it allows you to immediately deal with some practical problems that are frequently found when working on a facade. The different directions in the arrangement of the cubes in the space is not accidental; it allows you to test not only the method but also to clarify some very complex aspects.

The example differs from operating on the facade of a building for two main reasons:

- You can use any video projector: it is not necessary to calculate the optics and the distance because projectors for common use do not have interchangeable lenses; it is only necessary to verify empirically that the projector illuminates the scene completely.
- Given the small scale of the model is not necessary to rectify the photograph.

That said, it was decided to use the DLP Sharp PG-F312X projector with the following features: Resolution XGA: 1024x768, 3000 ANSI Lumens, 2200:1 contrast, lens ratio 1.8-2.1:1.

A scene type of different size cubes was used, arranged as in figure II.6 to form an angle, between the two arrangements, of 90°. The photo was shot from a height of about 1.70 m.

As the pyramid projection of this model of video projector is not centered relative to the lens (it is asymmetric), the picture projection is higher than its base and it creates a distance called offset, which depends on the distance at which the video projector is placed (figure II.7).

To reduce the offset and therefore be able to cover the base of the cubes with the projection, the projector was positioned as in figure II.8.

This positioning, even if it is unusual, is important in that it clarifies that in video mapping the correct display is only from the point of view from which the photo was taken, the location where the projector must be placed. This statement, from a teaching point of view, makes the reader check its accuracy, putting oneslef in a lower position and looking at the composition according to the right perspective. When the video projector is turned on and the zoom is positioned to wide (the setting to be kept during any exercise) you can verify that the scene is completely illuminated (figure II.9).

Figure II.6 – Structure created on cardboard cubes arranged in a general way in an indoor environment.

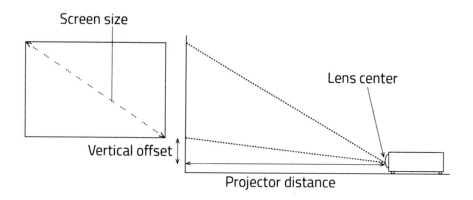

Figure II.7

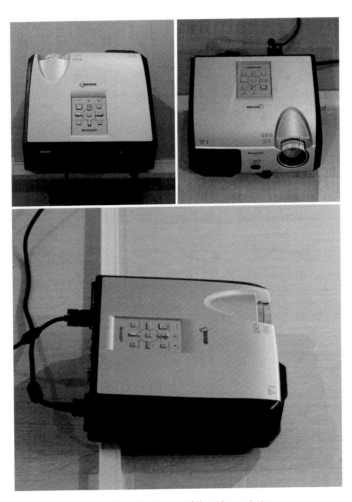

Figure II.8 – Positioning of the video projector.

The video projector has been positioned at a distance of 4.3 m and has generated a projection image with a height of 1.7 m and a width of 2.3 m (it should be emphasised that the zoom is positioned to wide).

Following one of the links listed below, and locating the make and model of the projector, it is possible to find all the information that is needed:

- http://www.projectorcentral.com/projection-calculator-pro.cfm
- http://www.schermionline.it/calcolo_distanze_videoproiettori_schermionline_it.html

Figure II.9 – Framing of the scene with the projector.

After placing the projector, a picture was taken by placing the camera directly above the lens of the projector (figure II.10).

Figure II.10 – Photograph taken by positioning the camera on the lens of the video projector.

The photograph was taken with a Canon Eos 600D and it generated a file of 5184x2812 pixels. The photograph, can later be scaled using Photoshop®, until reaching the aspect ratio of the video projector (in this specific case 1024x768 pixels) and cleaning up the background. These tasks will be addressed in detail in chapter 9. For now it is enough to know that for all the following work steps, the photo will be used as it appears in figure II.12, whose file was named **cubes_photo.jpg**.

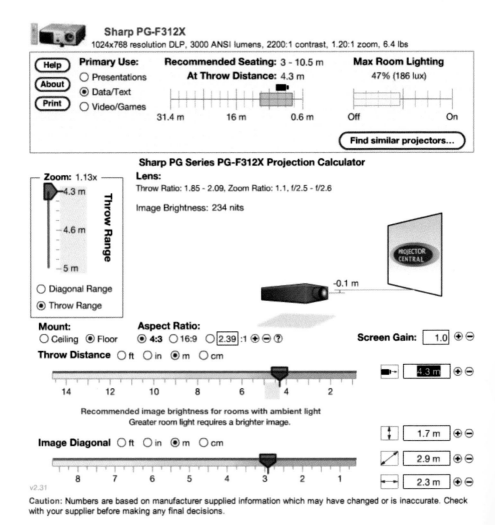

Figure II.11 – Screenshot taken from the website www.projectorcentral.com/ after entering the make and model of projector used in the appropriate fields.

Figure II.12 – cubes_photo.jpg. file.

Chapter 3

Architectural synthesis: creating layer masks in Illustrator®

Architecture is inhabited sculpture.

Constantin Brâncuși

Video mapping
performance,
(crew with
Vjzaria, Kalu and
Kanaka Project)
Oddstream
Festival, Nimega,
Holland, 2012

CHAPTER 3

3.1 Breaking down architecture into simple shapes: layer masks

The graphical translation of photographs into images is a very common theme to those who are preparing to work in the field of video mapping. To achieve such a task requires developing intuition or imaginative sensitivity which allows you to extract and reproduce a reality existing in three dimensional space on a two-dimensional surface. It is necessary to understand, in studying architecture, relationships between its elements and how to encapsulate the form so that it can then be designed as effects and interactions.

The discipline that allows the representation (through geometric constructions) of spatial forms in graphic images is descriptive geometry. It, through orthogonal projections, axonometry and perspective, is used to depict architecture and develop the sensitivity needed to mentally visualise and foresee what you will accomplish.

An initial way to familiarise yourself with architectural complexity is to analyse its components and break them down into simpler and more easily manageable elements. The photography of architecture contains a wealth of information, not all necessary, and the reconstruction into geometric shapes, passing from a photograph to its graphic representation, consisting of lines and closed forms, allows a formal summary from where to start the mapping process.

) mapping
rmance,
with
a, Kalu and
ka Project)
tream
val,
ga,
nd, 2012

When you start working on a rectified photograph it is appropriate to recreate the forms that simplify the complexity of the architectural structure, if any. For this reason it is useful to reconstruct the facade as if it were composed of many colour maps. This will be useful during the warping phase as it will allow you to work more easily with coloured references that replicate the homologous representation in reality. The colour maps take the name of "layer mask" and represent the digital reconstruction of the projection surface in sections. Depending on the complexity and type of design approach, various architectural parts will be modelled and this will allow the development of the project, from 3D to 2D animations. Layer masks represent the main reference file and will be reconstructed in Illustrator. The use of this software will allow the reconstruction and the export of each level which can then be animated in After Effects (Adobe technology allows easy interchange of files from one type of software to another, such as Photoshop ↔ Illustrator or Illustrator ↔ After Effects). With Illustrator you can manage the complex mapping file, which can be equipped with a very large number of layer masks (from a few dozen to a few hundreds), corresponding to the architectural elements of the facade that allow the creation of the animations.

Contrary to popular belief, in video mapping great precision is not always required in the reconstruction of the mapping file. The masks should settle "perfectly" on the surface, taking into account two variables that allow a degree of "relative accuracy": the distance of the projection relative to the spectator and the shape of the actual structure. Excessive zeal in the reconstruction of the elements of the structure, such as tracing many lines or not drawing them well, could increase the possibility of visual errors and problems in the exchange of files and/or in the 3D reconstruction. In the following figures the sense of synthesis necessary is indicated visually. As is clear, not all the lines have been reproduced (figures III.1, III.2 and III.3).

Figure III.1 – Cloister of San Francesco, Palazzo di Città, Ostuni (BR). Location of the first GLOWFestival.

Figure III.2 – Cathedral of San Sabino, Canosa di Puglia (BT).

Figure III.3 – Church of San Vito Martire, Ostuni (BR). Location of the second GLOWFestival.

3.2 Basic functions of Illustrator for video mapping

To successfully complete the reconstruction of the masks, the file named **cubes_photo. jpg** will be used as an example. The size will be set to the default resolution of the video projector in question (in the example a standard resolution XGA 1024x768 px was used).

Below is what to do step by step to create layer masks.
Open Illustrator and create a new file by setting the parameters of the project as follows:

1) Go to **File > New** to open a window as in figure III.4. Name the document and set the size of it (width and height), the colour mode (RGB is used because we are working in a video environment) and the resolution to 72 dpi. In this way the

photograph **cubes_photo.jpg**, which will be inserted, will match with the Artboard Tool created. Illustrator provides several functions for vector design, and the ability to work on multiple boards allows having multiple surfaces available on which to draw, therefore assessing the progress of the project.

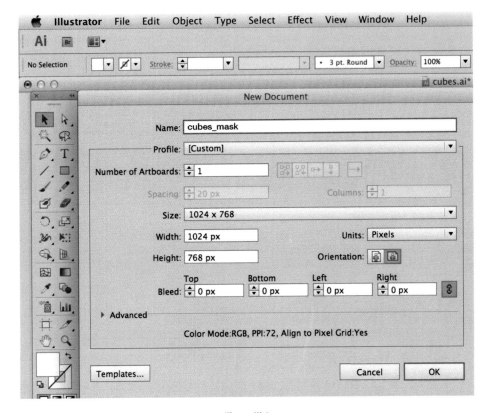

Figure III.4

2) Import the photograph (previously rectified in Photoshop) by going to **File > Place...** (figure III.5).

3) Before starting to draw the masks, you can customise the work interface by clicking on **Window** and selecting, if not already available, the items: **Layers, Align, Color**. These panels contain the functions to manage the masks individually and assign them to different levels so that they can be successfully exported. If the photo is not automatically centered on drawing board, use the *Align* command: click on **Align> Align to Artboard** and then align the photograph by clicking **Horizontal Align Centre and Vertical Align Centre** (figure III.6).

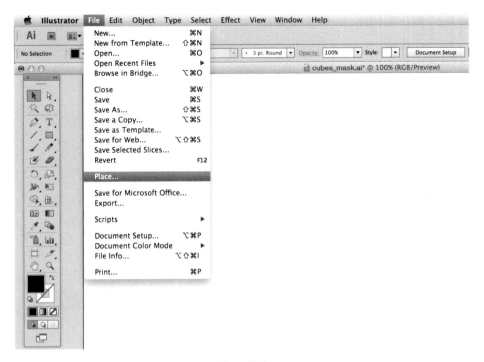

Figure III.5

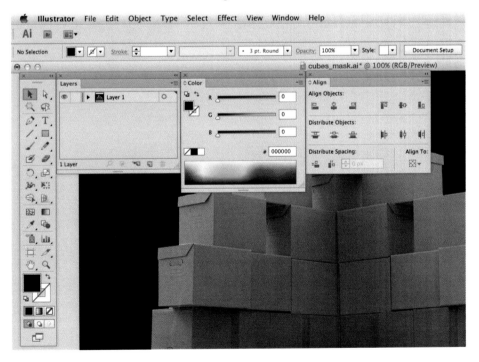

Figure III.6

4) After importing the file you should lock its position on the drawing board to prevent unwanted movements. You can use one of the keyboard shortcuts by pressing **cmd + 2** (Mac) to block the photograph. To unlock its position again press **shift + cmd + 2**. If you use a PC, replace the **cmd** key with **ctrl**. The two blue diagonals indicate that the photo is not included in the file. To avoid losing the connection to the photo, in case it is moved to another folder, include it in the file. To do this simply click once on the photo and then click on the word *Embed* that appears at the top. This done, the blue lines will disappear.

5) Select the *Pen Tool*, which allows you to draw the layer masks, draw straight and curved lines, add and delete points. Any operation is modifiable at any time. Start to trace the photograph as in figure III.7, creating a new Layer for every architectural element.

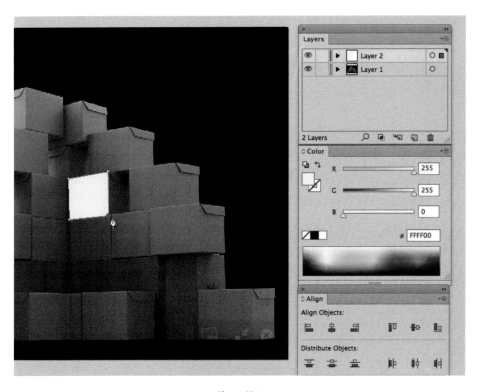

Figure III.7

In the **Layers** panel create a new level through the icon *New Layer* (figure III.8). For every single mask you must make a new layer. The order of the layers can be decided by simply dragging the level to be moved in the **Layers** panel, from top to bottom. To assign a colour to a layer mask, after having selected it, click on the colour bar in the **Color** panel (this gives a visual distinction to each architectural layer). Then continue to draw all the elements of the structure that are considered necessary.

The reconstruction should happen element by element, based on the features of the structure and its complexity. For every element or layer there should be a reference level.

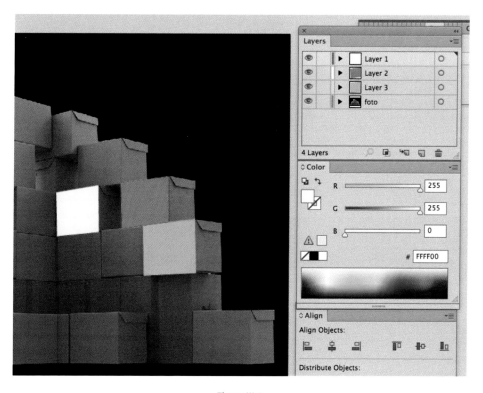

Figure III.8

Repeat the procedure for all the elements in the photograph and the result will be that shown in figure III.9.

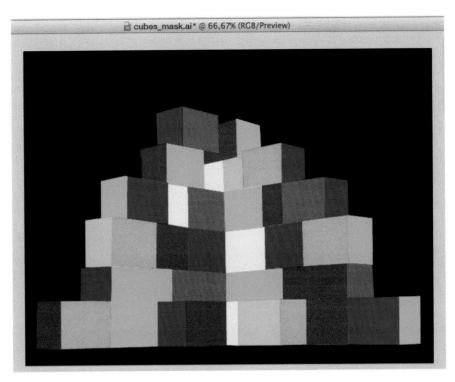

Figure III.9

What happens if the working file has all the masks on the same level?
The **Layers** panel can help through the option **Reverse to Layers** (sequence), activated by the Options icon on the top right of the **Layers panel** (figure III.10). This option allows the division of a single level of masks into a number of layers equal to them. After selecting the option, it will be observed that many other layers will be created from one single layer, based on the number of masks in the file. Simply drag the levels outside the main group and the file will be ready for exportation.

3.3 Export options for After Effects®

Once the reconstruction of the layer mask is finished, the file is ready to be exported to After Effects. Click on **File> Save As ...** (figure III.11), define the path to save the file which has been produced and rename it **cubes_mask.ai**. If you have multiple Artboards, you can select all or some during the save, depending on the shapes you want to export. Finally go to **Export ...** export the image to the colour map in .jpg format naming it **cubes.jpg**.

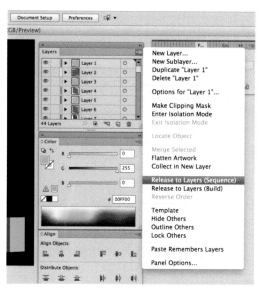

Figure III.10

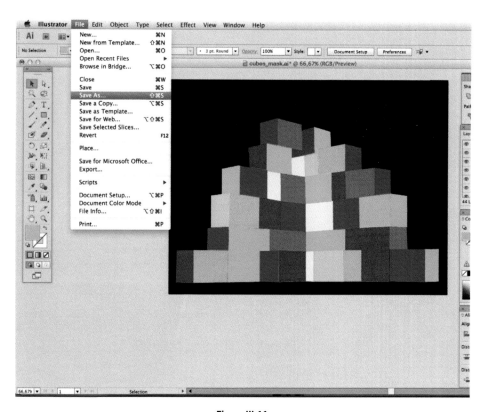

Figura III.11

Chapter 4

After Effects®: basic tool

for video mapping

Function, the use to which a work is put, isn't
enough, beauty is useful too.

Oscar Niemeyer

Les répétitions
de Figaro,
Video mapping
performance
competition,
Chartres en
lumieres,
France, 2013

CHAPTER 4

4.1 After Effects graphic interface

Having completed the reconstruction of the layer masks in Illustrator, and prepared them for exportation, the next step is importing the files into After Effects.

After Effects is professional software for graphic animation and video editing with advanced features, essential for the creation of content for mapping. It allows you to manage 2D animations and create a fake 3D effect of shadows and light by inserting a virtual camera. It allows you to import various file types, sequences of images, audio, animations and make a rough audio-video which is accurate enough to give you a good idea of the final design.

Below the creation of a new composition is covered and the basic interface is examined.

Open After Effects by clicking on **Composition > New Composition**. A window will open like that in figure IV.1 in which the parameters of the new composition, described below, will be set.

Preset: *Custom* – This parameter allows you to set customized options in the document.

Width: *1024 px & Height: 768 px* – These values refer to the output of the video projector or rather the resolution used by the rectified photograph. The software, once the values have been inserted, automatically recognises the aspect ratio. By blocking the proportion of the sides you can be certain that they will not be distorted by mistake while the composition is brought to life.

Pixel Aspect Ratio: *Square Pixels* – This option refers to the shape of the pixels, in this case square.

Frame Rate: *25 Fps* – The frequency of the frames corresponds to the number of frames per second.

Resolution: *Full* – This option refers to the quality of the preview video.

Start Timecode: *00:00:00:00* – This time value (hours:minutes:seconds:frames) refers to the start time of the the the animation.

Duration: *00:00:10:00* – Refers to the duration of the animation, in this case ten seconds.

Background Color: *Black* – This option allows the choice of the background colour of the animation.

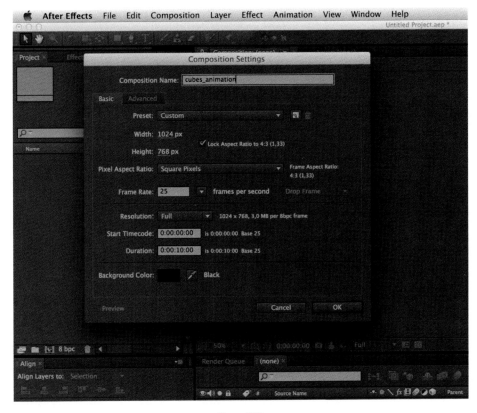

Figure IV.1

Once the parameters have been set, name the composition **cubes_animation** and click on **OK**; this done, the interface is shown as in figure VI.2. By clicking on **File > Save** it is possible to save the file and proceed to the choice of location to store the file. This file can be called **tutorial_AE.aep**.

Obviously all the parameters can be subsequently modified by going to **Composition > Composition Settings**.

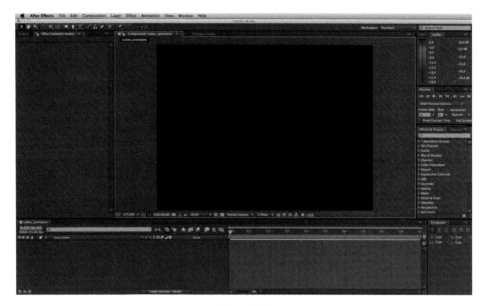

Figure IV.2

The standard interface of After Effects makes some essential panels available to the user to work with the created composition. It can be customised according to the needs of the project, activating the panels relating to the tools that you are interested in by clicking on **Window** shown in the toolbar.

4.2 Importing files

Having created the composition you can start to import the layer masks which were previously produced in Illustrator. To import them, click on **File > Import > File...** .
A window will open (figure IV.3) in which you can set the option as described below:

Enable: *All Acceptable Files* – This option allows the selection of the format of the file to be imported. After Effects automatically recognises the format of the file that is being imported and applies the specific options related to it.

Format: *Illustrator Pdf/Eps* – In the case that an Illustrator file is selected, After Effects directly recognises the format.

Import as: *Composition* – This option allows the choice of having the file in the format of the composition and/or individually, allowing the modification and animation of the layer masks which have been imported.

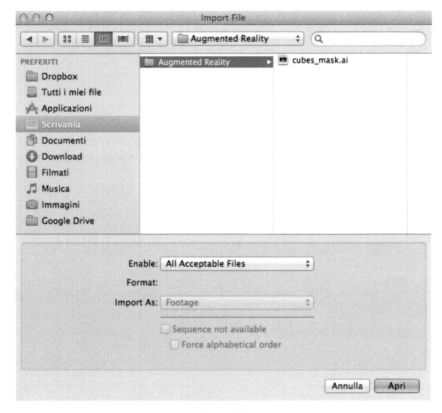

Figure IV.3

Once the files have been imported, you will note that in the **Project** panel (figure IV.4) three new folders are available: cubes (corresponding to the completed image of the structure), **cubes Layer** (containing all the individual layers reconstructed in illustrator) and **cubes_ animation** (relating to the current application).

Depending on the needs of the project and the animation that you want to achieve, you can select the entire reconstruction or a single mask and proceed to the importation in the composition.

Selecting the composition **cubes**, you can drag the entire image of the construction of the structure into the project. Instead, by opening the folder **cubes Layers** (figure IV.5) you can select and drag a single layer mask, previously reconstructed, into the project. In the event that you want to import multiple files you can use the convenient drag & drop function, dragging them one by one into the **Project** panel.

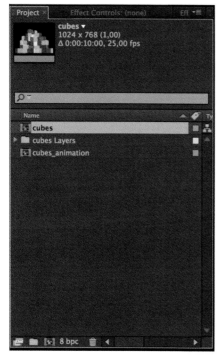

Figure IV.4

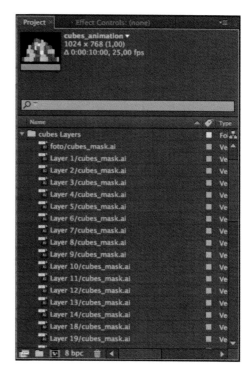

Figure IV.5

4.3 Key frame: the basics of animation

One aspect which is common to many versions of editing software is the use of key frames and the interpolation between them. The key frame is a type of frame that defines the start, end or middle state of a digital animation. In After Effects, you can animate any element that has as a stopwatch icon (figure IV.6-a). By clicking the stopwatch icon you activate the corresponding key frame (figure IV.6-b).

Figure IV.6

Having established the start and end key frames of a film, you can create intermediate frames manually or by interpolation. To manage the animation in After Effects, use the **Timeline** panel. First drag into the timeline the **cubes** composition and the five layers contained in the cubes Layer folder. On the timeline you will notice that After Effects has created on the preset time period a visual element that represents the period in which you can animate the layer (figure IV.7). The layers are manageable from the menu using the item **Layer**. The composition will be made up of six layers: the first is the reconstruction of the structure formed by all layer masks (on which will be applied a simple variation of opacity), while the other five are layer masks corresponding to the various faces of the cubes (on which will be applied a filter).

Figure IV.7

Assigning a colour to the layer label (by clicking on the box located next to the number of the layer itself), it will automatically be shown on the period of the timeline. This gives a visual separation of the elements so as to facilitate the user's orientation in projects with a high number of layers.

Selecting the layer and clicking on the arrow at the side of the colour label you can select a parameter to be animated and activate the key frames. Referring to the **cubes** layers, select the icon relating to the **Opacity** parameter= *100%*. By clicking the stopwatch icon you will notice that on the timeline, at zero seconds, a yellow diamond appears indicating the creation of a key frame, in this case the starting point of a key frame animation. Continuing on the timeline with the time slider, until the end of the animation, change the **Opacity** value to **0**. In correspondence with the change of value, it will automatically create another key frame. By clicking on the keyboard space bar or the **Play** button in the **Preview** panel you can see the result of the animation (you simply vary the opacity of the layer until it disappears entirely). Turning to the *Layer3/cubes_mask.ai* level, another effect can be applied and so on for all the other layer masks imported with the same options.

To apply an effect you need to select the **Effects & Presets** panel (figure IV.8) which contains a simplified collection of various preset effects and plug-ins. The panel shows a series of folders in which there are various categories of effects, from particle generation to cinematographic filter and, depending on your needs, you can use or modify one of the many presets available. The same effects in the **Effects & Presets** panel can be found by clicking on **Effect** on the toolbar at the top.

Figure IV.8

In this example, find the **Transition** folder, which contains transition effects. Select the *Venetian Blinds* effect and drag it onto the layer relating to the single mask named **Layer3/ cubes_mask.ai**. With the **Effect controls** panel open (figure IV.9), you will notice that the writing *fx* present within it is activated, indicating that the filter is active on the layer in question.

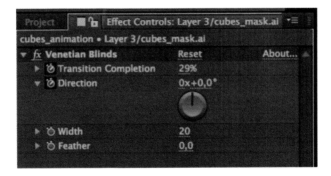

Figure IV.9

Through the **Effect Controls** panel you can set the animation parameters, always retrievable and modifiable from the submenu, also present into the timeline (figure IV.10). That said, go on to use the *Venetian Blinds* effect.

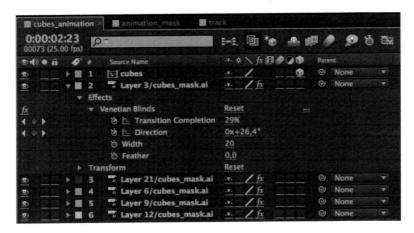

Figure IV.10

Having brought the time slider to the beginning of the timeline of the composition, click the stopwatch icon referring to the parameter **Transition Completion**, setting the start key frame. It is clear that, in this phase, if you simply push forward the time cursor on the composition, you will not notice any change on the layer mask.

Pushing the time slider to the end of the composition, and changing the value of **Transition Completion** from *0%* to *100%*, you will notice that the layer in question will disappear between oblique lines.

Repeat the operation done on this layer on the other imported layers (in this case the effect was added to the other four layers), varying the parameters and experimenting with the various options of the effect.

That done, to see the result, go back with the time slider and start the Preview, pressing the *Play* icon (figure IV.11 and IV.12).

Having applied two simple effects on six layers, you have achieved your first animation.

In the next paragraph the technique for creating some layer masks directly in After Effects, will be illustrated, managing the parameters and applying animation to achieve more videos to export.

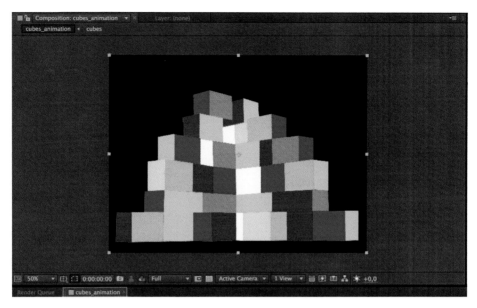

Figure IV.11 – Starting point (0:00:00:00 Transition Completion = 0%).

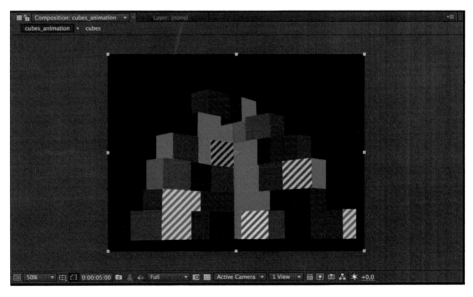

Figure IV.12 – Intermediate point (0:00:05:00 Transition Completion = 50%).

4.4 Creation and animation of layer masks

The same reconstruction of layer masks made in Illustrator can be obtained directly in After Effects, in that it has tools that are very similar to Illustrator.

The advantage of using Illustrator depends on the fact that it is a type of software specifically for vector graphics, and therefore beyond offering dedicated functionality, it allows you to easily trace hundreds of elements.

If you find yourself working on simple elements, it is possible to use only After Effects for the reconstruction of the layer masks.

Before creating an animation with a layer of the type **Solid** o **Shape Layer**, it is important to describe the tools **Rectangle Tool** ▨ and **Pen Tool** ▨, which will be used for the reconstruction of the layer masks.

Rectangle Tool – This tool allows the creation of a rectangle or other geometrical shape, that can be animated and managed like layer masks, as has been seen before.

Pen Tool – This tool, together with the Rectangle Tool will be one of the basic tools for the creation of layer masks. It is characterised by the same functionality seen in Illustrator, for its design and management.

Create a new composition by clicking on **Composition > New Composition**, leaving the options unchanged, calling it animation_mask and importing the **cubes_photo.jpg** file that will be used for reference. To create a **solid** layer, click on the options **Layer > New > Solid** (figure IV.13).

In this phase you can decide the parameters to assign (figure IV.14): name (mask_1), size and colours to associate to the solid. The solid created will fill all the work area, so in order to have a visual reference of the image, reduce the opacity of the layer using the submenu shown on the timeline.

Keeping the layer selected, click on the Pen Tool and draw a layer mask on an element of the composition (figure IV.15).

In this way a layer has been created on the element (figure IV.16); in the submenu of the layer **mask_1** a new item called **Masks** will be shown on the timeline, containing the mask you have just created.

With this operation you have transformed the solid which was originally rectangular into a defined form, in this case it refers to the face of a cube in the structure.

Click on the **Pen Tool** and, without deselecting the layer, draw a form inside the layer *mask_1*. The mask that has just been created will simply be added to the previous one without producing any effect (figure IV.17).

Figure IV.13

Figure IV.14

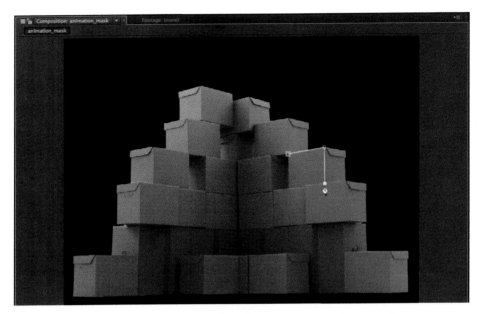

Figure IV.15

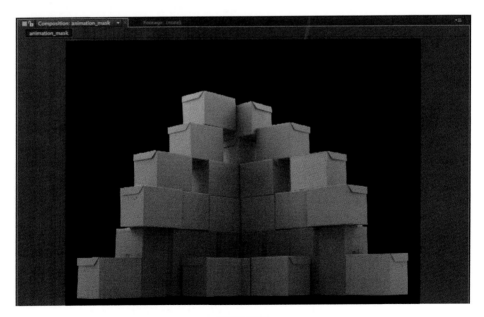

Figure IV.16

It will be necessary to define the method of intersection by going to modify it in the submenu **Masks**. Selecting **Subtract** on the second rectangle, as in figure IV.18.a, achieves the result in figure IV.18.b.

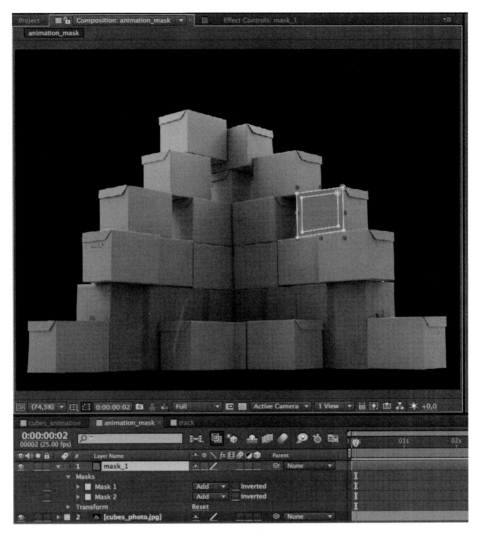

Figure IV.17

Figure IV.18.a

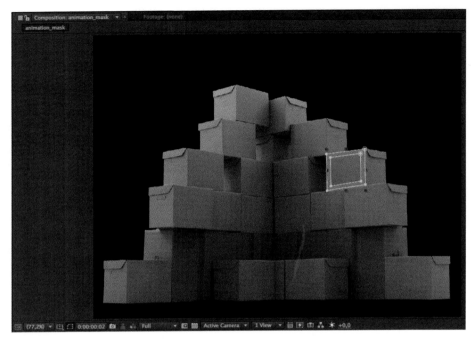

Figure IV.18.b

Once the way to create a layer mask from a solid is understood, you can also make a reconstruction of layer masks similar to that of figure IV.19 – or following your own logic and inspiration – containing more solids differing from each other in colour or shape.

You can now create an animation and apply it to the layer masks, in the same or a different way, depending on the results you want to achieve.

Select the **Linear Wipe** effect from the **Effects & Presets > Linear Wipe** and drag it onto ono of the layer masks you have made.

In the parameters of the **Linear Wipe** effect (figure IV.20), click on **Transition Completion**. In this way you create a key frame, for example in the time position of 0 seconds. Then move the time slider halfway along the time bar (00:00:05:00) of the composition and set the value of the Transition Completion at **100%**.

For the **Wipe Angle** parameter, which managers the transition angle, the same procedure can be followed where it is thought to be appropriate.

Having achieved the animation of a mask, the **Linear Wipe** effect can be applied to the other masks, dragging it or copying it from the animation – selecting on the timeline the effect show in the submenu of the layer just animated – and pasting it on the chosen mask. Once the effect has been pasted you can modify or leave unchanged the animation parameters.

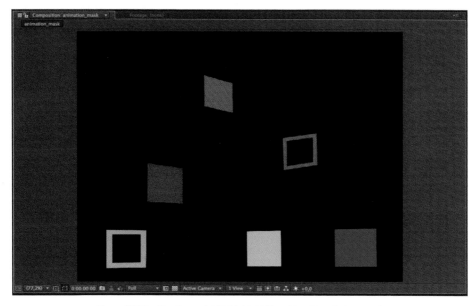

Figure IV.19 – Starting point (0:00:00:00 Transition Completion = 0%).

Before carrying out the copy-paste, it is necessary to check whether the key frame of the parameter that has been animated (in this case **Transition**) is selected and active (coloured yellow). To copy the effect just use the keyboard shortcut **Cmd+C** (Mac) or **Ctrl+C** (PC), while to paste it select the layer on which you want to apply the effect and use **Cmd+V** (Mac) o **Ctrl+V** (PC).

With this operation, a clone of the first animation is obtained, which can be used as a base on which to create some corresponding transitions or as a final animation for the reference layer.

Following the criteria outlined, apply animation to each of the layer masks shown and, through the preview, check the result obtained (figure IV.21).

Finally, continue save the composition through **File > Save**.

Figure IV.20

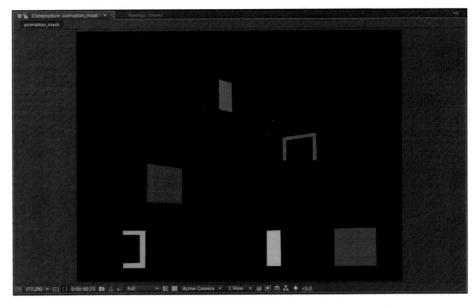

Figure IV.21 – Intermediate point (0:00:00:23 Transition Completion = 48%).

Up until now you have seen how to create some layer masks and animate them with the *Solid* option. After Effects has other drawing tools which are useful for layer masks. Therefore, before proceeding to export the animation, the *Shape Layer* option will be discussed.

The *Shape Layer* option is very similar to the *Solid* option – from the point of view of functionality – but offers greater customisation in the phases of creation, design and of applying some of the effects.

Accordingly, create a new composition in the project named **track**, clicking on **Composition> New Composition** and importing the file **cubes_photo.jpg** that will be used for reference. Within this composition create a new layer *Shape Layer* by clicking on **Layer> New Layer> Shape Layer** (figure IV.22).

Figure IV.22

For the *Shape Layer* you can decide if it should have the function of a mask or of a graphic object, choosing the graphics styles of the filling/stroke and some specific effects.

Of course, any compositions created earlier can be reopened at any time from the **Project** panel or by accessing them from the tabs in the **Timeline** panel.

The **Shape Layer** option creates an invisible surface on the composition. Activating it makes the *Pen Tool* cursor appear, with which you can draw any outline of the structure of the cubes, taking care not to ever deselect the layer.

In the options (figure IV.23.a), set the value of the **Stroke** to 4 px, i.e. the thickness of the line, and after clicking on the word **Fill** choose from the panel (figure IV.23.b) "no fill", clicking on its icon (white rectangle with a red diagonal). Create the outer outline of the **Shape Layer** as before (figure IV.24) and continue the reconstruction of the different facades of the cubes, to obtain a result similar to that of figure IV.25.

Figure IV.23.a

Figure IV.23.b

During the reconstruction phase of the layer masks, attention must be paid that the layer **Shape Layer** is always selected; in this way the faces which are reconstructed will always refer to the original layer in the **Contents** option (figure IV.26).

The reconstruction of the structure is fully editable both globally and in the case that you want to work on every single mask of the layer. This means that the option **Shape Layer** may be modified with the addition of new elements or deleting existing ones at any time.

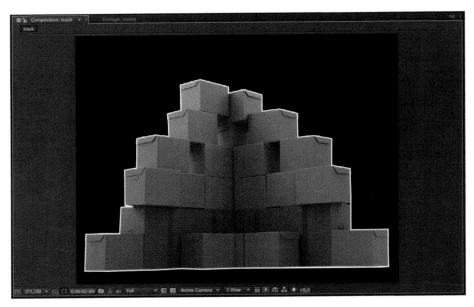

Figure IV.24

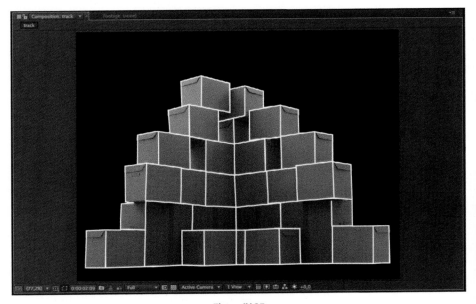

Figure IV.25

Once the reconstruction is complete, a global effect can be applied: drag the **Linear Wipe** effect from the **Effects & Presets** panel onto the layer **Shape Layer**.

Clicking on the **Transition Completion** parameter, create a key frame at the time of 0 seconds (figure IV.27). Move the time slider to the end (00:00:10:00) of the composition and set the value of Transition Completion to 100%.

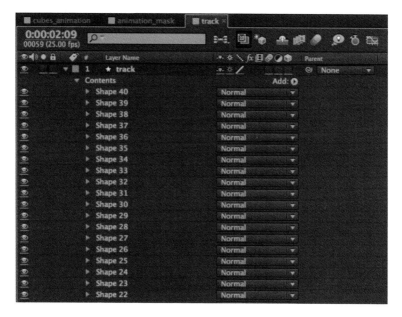

Figure IV.26

The same operation performed for the **Transition Completion** is carried out on the **Wipe Angle** parameter, setting the start of the key frames to the angular value of 0° and the last key frame to the value of 90°.

At this point check what has been done by going back on the timeline and playing a preview of the animation (figures IV.27 and IV.28). Save the composition by clicking on **File> Save**.

With the settings given, an animation has been created which is very similar to what can be achieved through **Trapcode STROKE3D®**, a famous plug-in for After Effects, an animation which is very well used by Pablo Valbuena (see Chapter 1) in many of his performances. **Trapcode STROKE3D**, developed by Red Giant[13], is very well known in the context of video mapping and it is used to create animations of lines and contours in space.

---

13. http://www.redgiant.com/products/all/trapcode-3d-stroke/

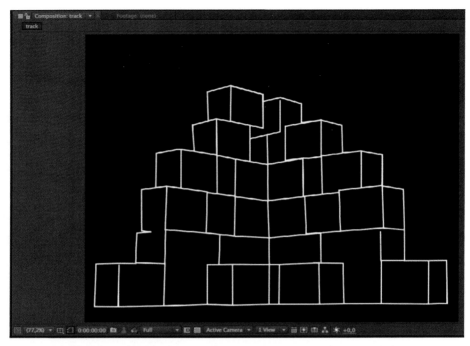

Figure IV.27 – Starting point (0:00:00:00 Transition Completion = 0% Wipe Angle = 0°).

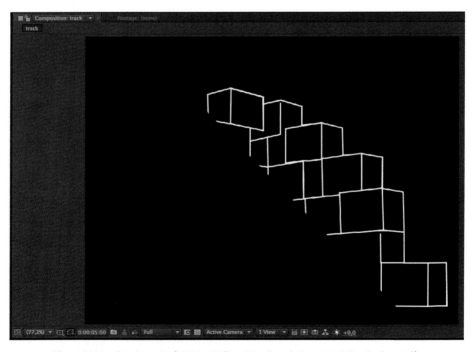

Figure IV.28 – Starting point (0:00:05:00 Transition Completion = 50% Wipe Angle = 45°).

4.5 Basic filters: Corner Pin and Mesh Warp

In order that created animations can settle on the faces of the cubes, to correct the distortions that can occur, you must use filters that allow a distortion of the animations on surfaces placed in an arbitrary way, which should ensure that they are adapted to a particular perspective. After Effects has two filters available for this purpose; the **Corner Pin** and the **Mesh Warp**. To implement this technique, you can import a video to distort the surfaces of the cubes to create a new animation on existing content.

Open the composition **cubes_animation** and import a video by clicking on **File > Import**. Once the video has been re-dimensioned, activate the first filter on the **Effects & Presets** panel, **Distort** folder, and drag the filter **Corner Pin** onto the Layer Video just imported (figure IV.29.a).

On the layer in question some blue pins are activated, on the four vertices, (figure IV.29.b) that allow the distortion in the perspective of the video (or any possible mask created).

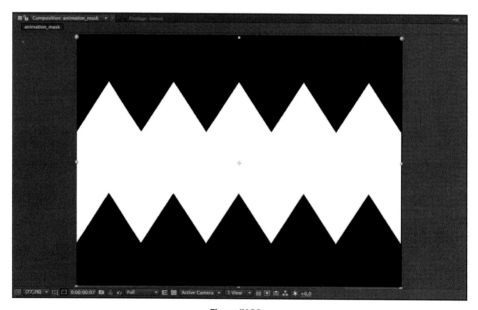

Figure IV.29.a

Figure IV.29.b

Working on the four vertices, it is in fact possible to distort the perspective (figures IV.30.a and

IV.30.b), obtaining as a result that shown in figure IV.31, that is the video perfectly matched to one of the faces of a cube.

Figure IV.30.a

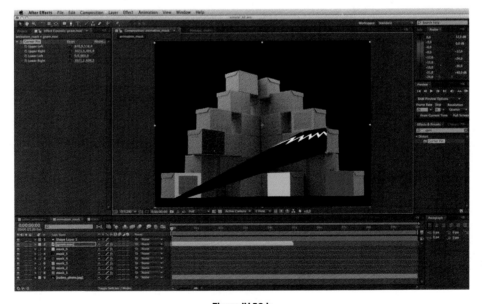

Figure IV.30.b

The *Corner Pin* filter can then be used to carry out warping (a technique for distorting images or video which is indispensable in video mapping) on some existing videos or to create new combinations of animations. It can also be controlled from the Effect Controls panel, though the manual setting of the four values corresponding to the co-ordinates of the vertices. (figure IV.32).

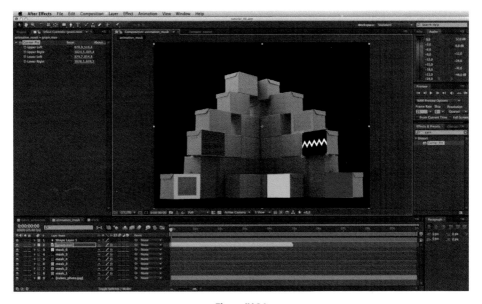

Figure IV.31

fx Corner Pin 2	Reset	About...
Upper Left		461,0,66,0
Upper Right		898,0,60,0
Lower Left		460,0,466,0
Lower Right		902,0,468,0

Figure IV.32

Clearly the operation described must be repeated on each element to be distorted.

After the change in perspective with the *Corner Pin* filter, the *Mesh Warp* filter can be used for the perfection of any details (figure IV.33).

The *Mesh Warp* filter allows you to perform the warping thanks to the subdivision of the layer into rows and columns (figure IV.34). This subdivision generates the mesh, that is a lattice that is usually rectangular, with which it is possible to move both the vertices and the intermediate points.

105

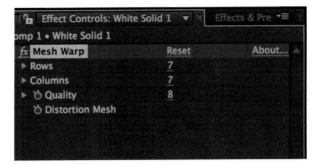

Figure IV.33

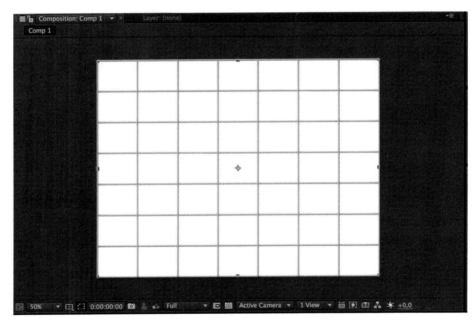

Figure IV.34

Selecting one of the points of the mesh, you can go on to move it or create curvilinear distortion in the area of interest (figure IV.35 a-b).

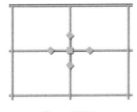

Figure IV.35.a

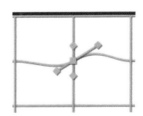

Figure IV.35.b

4.6 Simulating a 3D environment and virtual lighting

After Effects is designed for working with video objects and 2D animations and allows the simulation of a 3D environment with light and shade as well as the possible inclusion of one or more virtual rooms.

The potential of these tools is varied, especially when using some plug-in elements that transform light into spectacular effects. These plug-ins allow you, thanks to the use of the virtual camera, to travel inside the video and animation with zoom and changes in range.

A good mastery of the use of the simulation of a 3D environment allows you to obtain, in some cases, results very similar to those that you might have with the use of a specific 3D graphics software (Cinema 4D or similar) but in a decidedly simpler way.

To understand when you can simulate a 3D environment it is necessary to understand how After Effects runs this simulation.

Going to and activating the **3D Layer** icon (represented by the cube on a layer in the timeline), the software will provide the user, as in theatre scenery, several layers of varying depth.

To create a new light you must assign to the desired layer the option which allows 3D manipulation. For the light to function properly it needs to act in three dimensions, so as to recreate the effect of depth and perspective as happens in reality. The option that allows the insertion of the lights is called **3D Layer** and it must be activated for each level to which you want to apply a 3D manipulation.

In this case open the composition *Cubes_Animation* in the **Project** panel and enable the option *3D Layer* on the **Cubes** layer, which depicts the complete structure of the cubes.

At this point you can insert the light layer from the **Layer > New > Light** menu and set the parameters (listed below) as in figure IV.36.

Light Type – Allows you to decide what type of light to choose and, depending on the type of light, various options will be available.

Color – Allows the choice of the colour of the light.

Intensity – Adjusts the intensity of the light.

Cone angle – Option available for spot lights, defines the angle of projection.

Cone Feather – Option available for spot lights, regulates the shading of the light projection.

Falloff – Indicates dimming or decreasing of brightness moving away from the light source.

Cast Shadows – If chosen, activates the shadows deriving from the light.

Shadow Darkness – indicates the brightness of the shadow.

Shadow Diffusion - Adjusts the size of the spread of the shadows on the surface.

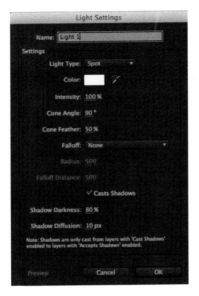

Figure IV.36

In figure IV.37 you can see the result of using a light with the parameters set as in figure IV.36.

The **Light 1** layer can be treated like all the other layers in After Effects. A submenu is shown on the timeline (figure IV.38), carrying the options set when creating the element.

Like all the other elements in After Effects, the **Light** option can be used to create some animations. **Point of Interest** can be used to create a movement of light effect.

This parameter shows three values that represent the position of the point of interest of the light on the axis X, Y and Z, allowing you to decide the position in the 3D environment created.

Activate the key frame of the **Point of Interest** parameter at the starting point and, varying the central value, referring to the Y axis, on the timeline in intervals of 3 seconds, you can set a light movement on the structure that will create a simulation of light and shade on it.

Going back to the timeline, you can play the Preview of the animation.

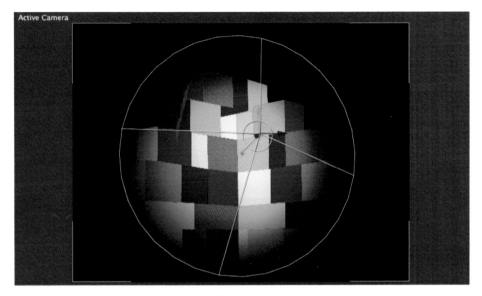

Figure IV.37

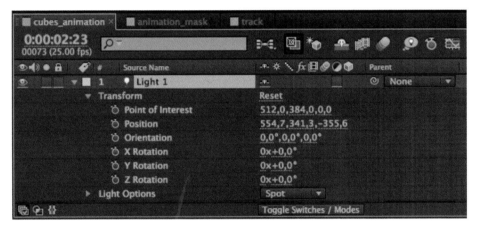

Figure IV.38

The animation of the **Point of Interest** creates a visual animation giving a reference to the light movement in the 3D environment and allows modification in the frames of interest, even by manual movement. Just move the centre point, which is on a grip, to manually edit the animation (figures IV.39, IV.40, IV.41, IV.42).

Having created the animations it is necessary to export the film by making a rendering. Rendering an animation allows for interchange so you can use the video you have generated in other software to play it, edit it, mount it etc.

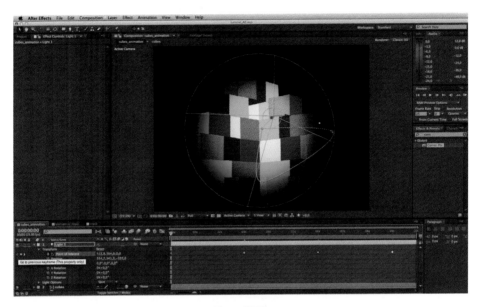

Figure IV.39

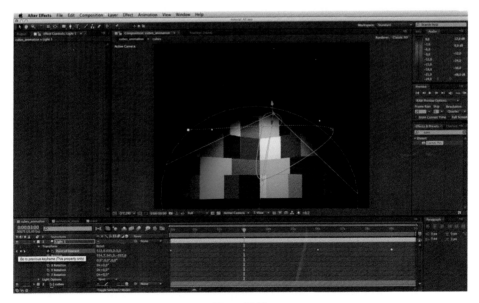

Figure IV.40

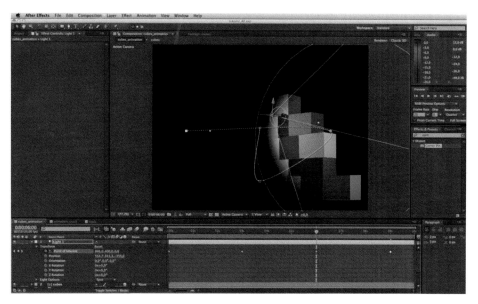

Figure IV.41

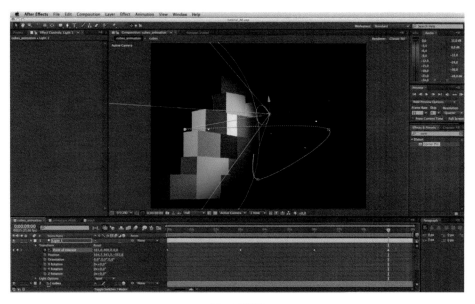

Figure IV.42

The rendering of a frame is a two dimensional image that includes all the parameters and settings of the composition from which it was generated; consequently the rendering of a film will consist of a set of the renderings of all the frames.

After achieving the required animation, you have to decide which, and how many, levels to render for the final output. The selection can be made with the icon relating to the layer visibility that allows you to hide or show the layers of the output.

Another manageable parameter is the time duration. To set the output sequence on the timeline, use as a visual reference the Time Toolbar, changing it from 10 seconds to 5 seconds (figure IV.43).

Moving the slider to the start or end, you can decide the beginning and the end of the animation, a time change that will be maintained even in the rendering phase. You can also change the duration retrospectively during the choice of output parameters.

Figure IV.43

Once the composition of the layers is decided, render two of the three sequences produced (animation mask and track).

To render the compositions with After Effects, click on **Composition > Add to Render Queue** (figure IV.44).

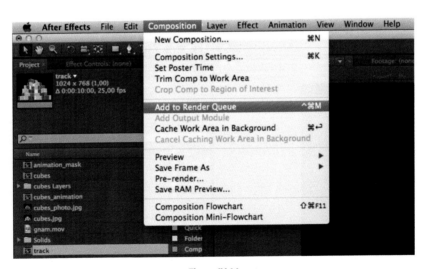

Figure IV.44

The file will be put in a queue and in the *Render Queue* tab, shown on the timeline, you can see the options for output. From the *Render Queue* tab we can always set all the features of the output, from the codec to the time duration, from the audio export to the frame rate.

In the **Render Queue** panel, three areas of changeable options are available: *Render Settings*, *Output Module* and *Output To* (figure IV.45).

Figure IV.45

Render Settings (→ Best settings) (figure IV.46) allows you to change the video quality, resolution, time duration and frame rate.

Figure IV.46

It is necessary to set the parameters of the *Render Settings* properly according to the type of output and it is essential to check that the *Frame Rate* is consistent with the value set initially (25 fps). Following carefully the example of this paragraph, you will have a duration equal to 00: 00: 05: 00.

The **Output Module Settings** panel (→ Lossless) (figure IV.47) allows complete management of the parameters of the image output: the choice of format, the video codec and the related channels, the incorporation of audio, of the general quality of the video, the resolution, the time duration and the frame rate. The options available for the various categories can be activated through a check box, positioned next to the name of the area itself.

Figure IV.47

Below are the options of the **Output Module Settings**, describing their meanings and stating the values chosen for the videos in this example.

Format: *QuickTime* – Shows the type of file format which is used in this case

Channel: *RGB* – Shows the colour mode. Choose RGB as it is the standard colour method intended for display on a monitor; do not incorporate the Alpha channel because the codec (DXV) that will be used later does not support that option.

Depth: *Millions of Colors* – Shows the depth of colours. In this case you need excellent video quality.

When you have set these parameters, it is necessary to click on the **Format Options**; a window opens (figure IV.48) in which it is possible to choose the codec to assign to the video and its quality. Use the **Photo-JPEG** codec, which will allow you to obtain an excellent quality video with little compression (that can be converted afterwards to the DXV codec through MPEG Streamclip – see chapter 6) and you can set the video quality to 100% (you can reduce it to 75% but you should not go beyond this). Even though it is possible to set the DXV codec in After Effects, it is better to convert it later.

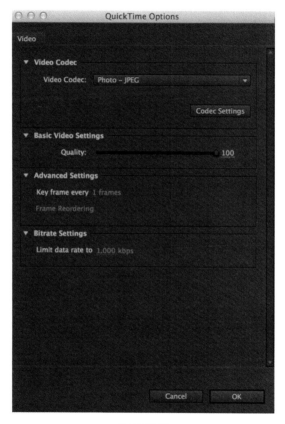

Figure IV.48

The **Output to** panel allows you to choose the location in which to save the video and name it.

After verifying that the parameters are correctly set, proceed to exportation by clicking on the *Render* button (figure IV.49). The progress of the exportation can be verified on the rendering toolbar as shown in the figure. On this toolbar you can also see the progress of the render and the advancement of the animation.

Depending on the type of image processing, the rendering stage may last from a few seconds to a few hours, meaning that the computer cannot be used during this operation. This suggests that it is always important to evaluate carefully, based on its intended use, the type of parameters to be used to render a video.

After concluding the rendering phase, the software will confirm its completion through a default sound and will update the information in the **Render Queue** panel.

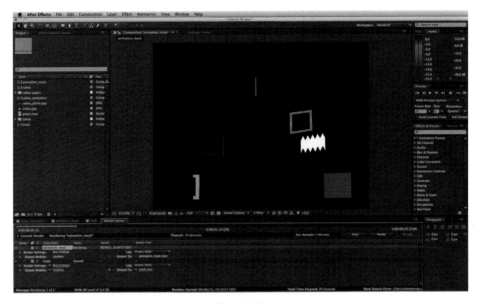

Figure IV.49

You have obtained a video in **QuickTime** format with the following features: **1024x768 pixels**, **Photo-JPEG** codec, duration **5 seconds**, frame rate **25 fps**.

Following the same procedure, opening the compositions you created before, you can export more videos.

Once you have created two animations (animation mask.mov and track.mov) you can use them to carry out a simple audio-video montage as described in chapter 6.

All the knowledge acquired in this chapter, enabling a basic approach to After Effects, can be used to achieve some digital reconstructions and manage animations choosing more parameters, in order to have some files to interchange between the various types of software.

Finally it should be noted that in the new versions of After Effects and 4D Cinema a plug-in is available that specifically enables the management of 3D files from 4D Cinema in After Effects.

Maxon Cineware not only allows you to import native Cinema 4D scenes, but also to use the workflow multi-pass as layers to make compositions.

The complete importation options of Cinema 4D allow the use of 3D objects in many of the more common exchange formats (Alembic, collada, obj, fbx etc.). It is possible to use it to create new cinema scenes directly in After Effects CC and that allows a quicker workflow for the mapping and, in particular, the stage mapping in that the rendering engine in Cinema is integrated with Adobe After Effects CC. After Effects can carry out the rendering of files produced with Cinema 4D and allow the control of some options for rendering, video camera and scene content in single levels. This optimised workflow does not require neither the creation of more intermediate passages nor image sequence files.

Chapter 5

Cinema 4D® : basic tool

for video mapping

Those who plan know to have reached perfection not
when there is no longer anything to add, but when
there is no longer anything to take away.

Antoine de Saint-Exupery

Butterflight
effect, Video
mapping
performance
completion,
Next Step Festival,
Milan, 2012.

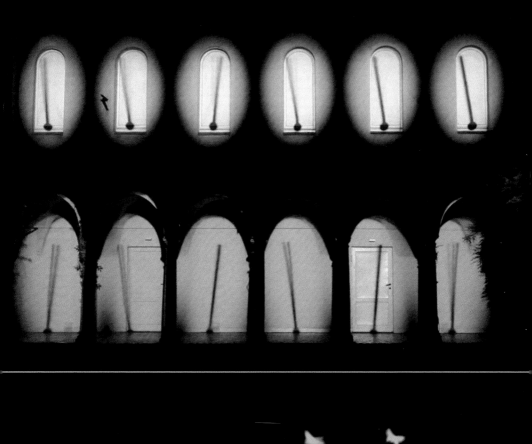

CHAPTER 5

5.1 Creating a 3D scene and Camera Calibration

To give substance and three dimensionality to the scenes that you intend to produce, it is necessary to make use of 3D graphics software.

Cinema 4D® is an excellent ally for the creation and management of three-dimensional effects. It supports procedural modelling techniques, polygonal and solid, the creation and application of textures, lighting management, animation and final rendering.

This chapter deals with the complex, but not difficult phase, when we will proceed to the reconstruction of a 3D environment with Cinema 4D, using the real scene obtained by the rectified photograph as reference (see Chapter 9).

One of the most frequent difficulties for those approaching video mapping for the first time is how to insert a three-dimensional model into a real context of which you have photographs. The purpose of this operation is precisely inserting the reconstructed three-dimensional scene in the photograph, respecting the perspective and proportions between the parts. For this to happen it is necessary to identify the exact point from which the photo was taken, so as to determine the right point for a correct perspective rendering.

The operation is called **Camera Matching** or **Camera Mapping** and each type of 3D software has its own procedure and specific commands to use it. Certainly personal skills and experience in managing and seeing the vantage point can be of great help.

Returning to the Cinema 4D software, it is interesting to note that it features a specific tag called *Camera Calibration*, to associate with the camera that performs this function.

The interface of Cinema 4D is very simple: the main screen initially consists of a single view but can be divided into four windows so you can manage multiple views, just as when working with the orthogonal projections (figure V.1).

terflight
ct, Video
ping
formance
pletion,
t Step
tival,
n, 2012.

121

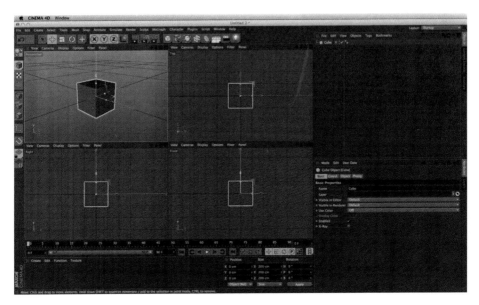

Figure V.1

The software handles two types of reference systems: one local and one global. Taking for example the cube shown in figure V.1, notice that it has a local reference system formed by three axes oriented orthogonally to one another: x (red → base), y (green → height), z (blue → depth). Initially, the local reference system of the cube coincides with the global reference system; this aspect is crucial for the management of the *Camera Calibration*.

After opening Cinema 4D, the first task to carry out is to set the project file and prepare the animation.

Click on **Edit > Project Setting** and in **Attribute Manager** the relevant window will appear (figure V.2). To produce an animation of ten seconds, the value in the *Maximum Time* field should be set to **250 F**.

The next step consists of setting the scene at the same resolution and output format of the projector and the related mapping file. Click on the icon *Edit Render Setting* as in figure V.3 to access the panel.

From the **Render Settings** panel, you can manage the output resolution and format. Since you have the mapping file with a resolution of 1024x768 px as a reference, set the values as follows:

Width: *1024 px*

Height: *768 px*

Lock Ratio: *ticked* (locks the proportions between the sides)

Resolution: *72 dpi*

Film Aspect: *4:3*

Pixel Aspect: *1*

Frame rate: *25 fps*

Frame range: *All frame – From = 0 F To = 250 F*

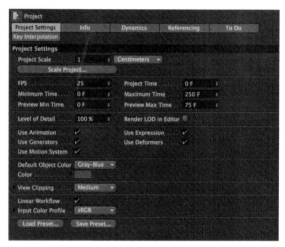

Figure V.2

Figure V.3

After setting the values, just confirm to close the window.

Having completed this, you must set the process that will allow you to align a real photo with a virtual model. Click on the camera icon to add a new one and the window will appear as in figure V.4.

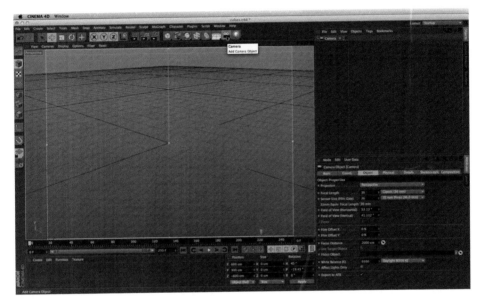

Figure V.4

The camera icon will appear in the **Object Manager**, its features in the **Attribute Manager** and the area of interaction will be visible in the **Render viewport**.

Often those new to video mapping wonder if you have to set the same perspective as the projector on the virtual camera. There are various theories that you can find online which actually hardly ever give a practical response.

In Cinema 4D the virtual camera settings are changed automatically when the **Camera Calibration** is carried out, so the process is much simpler than you might imagine. To do this, click with the right mouse button on **Camera> CINEMA 4D Tags> Camera Calibration** (figure V.5) and this will activate the icon to the right of the camera.

You must now go to the settings panel for **Camera calibration** and load the image **cubes_ photo.jpg**. Having done this, the image will appear in the work area (figure V.6).

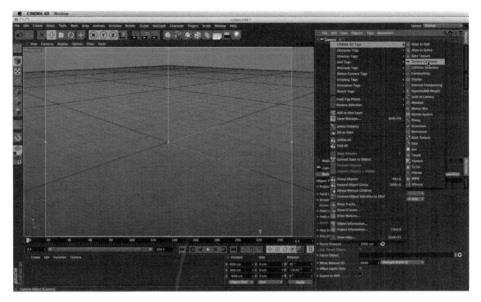

Figure V.5

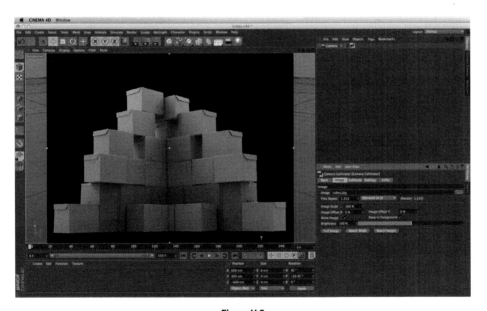

Figure V.6

To help the reader understand the working mechanism of **Camera Calibration**, we will briefly try to provide the basic concepts of descriptive geometry. For this purpose the cube of figure V.7 is used as a reference, whose perspective is defined by lines that converge at points A and B. The more accidental the perspective, the more it will be easy to identify these points as they will tend to approach the Horizon Line (HL).

The *Camera calibration*, in reality, follows the same reconstruction of figure V.7. Cinema 4D identifies how many more perspective lines are possible on the image, which help to define the axis (HL) of the perspective and according to these proceeds to the insertion of the virtual camera. From the picture, therefore, the unique position of the camera from which the perspective mentioned above is visible is identified in as precise a way as possible.

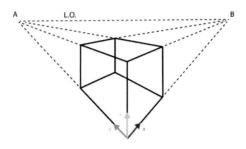

Figure V.7

Through the **Calibrate** command (figure V.8) the software offers three different tools to determine the perspective (Line, Grid, Pin) that can be used alone or combined with each other. The more complex the perspective, the greater the number of additional tools on which you can rely. Generally, with just the lines a correct perspective can be identified.

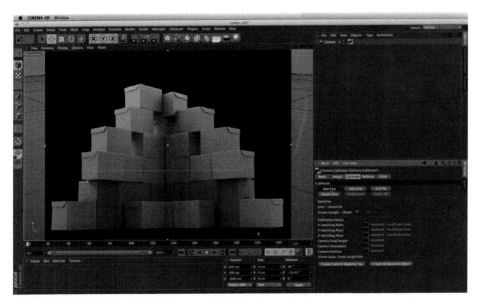

Figure V.8

Clicking on **Calibrate > Add Line**, a line will appear; supposing that you want to determine the x axis, you arrange the line according to the perspective lines identified from the image. To have a greater degree of precision you can temporarily enlarge the ends of the line inserted (figure V.9).

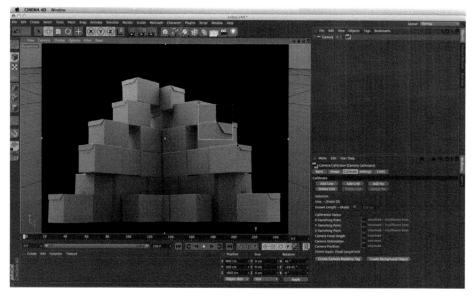

Figure V.9

Having defined the correct perspective of the line, you can specify which axis should correspond to it by clicking on it while holding down the Shift key simultaneously (both mac users both PC users). During this operation, the central part of the line will be coloured red, indicating that the software is asking if you want to associate the x axis. Follow the same procedure for the other axes that will be coloured in the middle respectively green, (y → height) and blue (z → depth).

Defining the other lines (figure V.10), as soon as the software has identified the x-axis, the square to the right of X **Vanishing Point** will turn green. The search for the x-axis must, of course, also be made for the other two axes (figure V.11).

In the event that you are faced with a complex perspective, as in the case in question, the software has difficulty in identifying the points of convergence (in this case a yellow square appears as shown in figure V. 11). This does not mean that the task is impossible. Where, using just the lines, Cinema 4D is not able to locate the proper perspective, you can make use of plans and points.

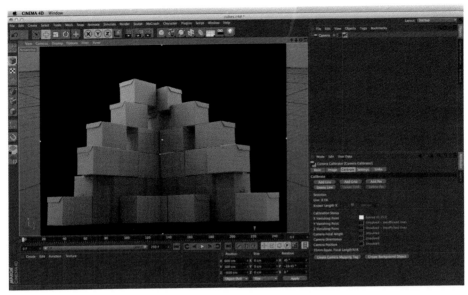

Figure V.10

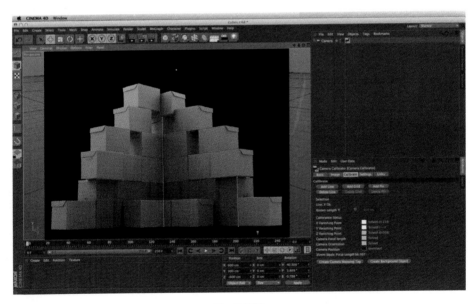

Figure V.11

Having identified the perspective all you have to do is to click on **Create Background Object** (the function that transforms photography into virtual background) and on **Create Tag Mapping Camera** (the function that creates the virtual camera).

Clicking on the camera icon shown in figure V.12, you will notice that, by the mouse pointer, the background grid (the one behind the photograph) changes its position in the space placing itself at the bottom. This means that the position of the virtual camera in space has been identified and that it "coincides" with the point of view from which the photograph was taken. This position, in principle, also represents the point of view of the projector, but the perfect match will happen subsequently during the warping phase.

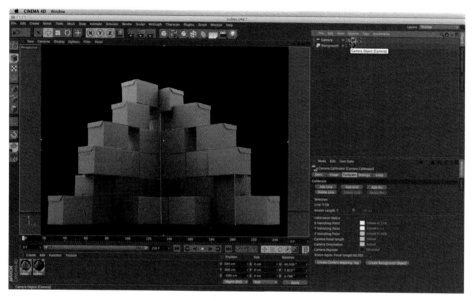

Figure V.12

At this point nothing else is left but to insert the cubes as in figure V.13, which will be automatically placed in the correct perspective; then you will have to distort them to make them take on the form of parallelepipeds.

To place the cubes in the space it is useful to display multiple screens again, activated by clicking on **Panel> All view**, or by clicking on the appropriate icon.

To modify the size of the inserted cubes quickly, you can make use of the yellow grips placed on their vertices, and to move them easily in the space while looking at the photo below, you should activate the **X-Ray** function on the *Basic* tab on the **Cube** panel (figure V.14). As with the first cube you will need to repeat the steps above for all cubes inserted in the scene (figure V.15).

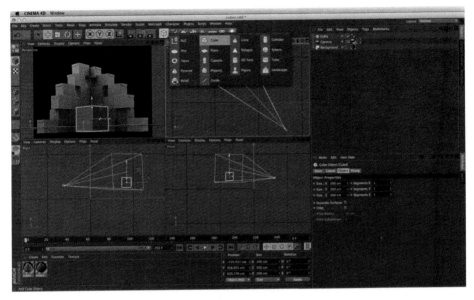

Figure V.13

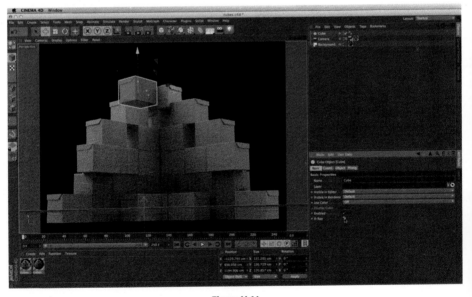

Figure V.14

It will be observed that the camera is positioned low down exactly in the position imagined. This position coincides with that from which the photo was taken.

After inserting all the cubes and distorting and repositioning them, the result will be similar to that of figure V.16. To have the same view as that in the figure it is necessary to click on **Render> Render View**, or on the appropriate icon ![icon] .

It is interesting to note that any object which is inserted into the scene will respect the viewpoint and will be consistent with the scene itself. The scene then becomes the reference on which to carry out any procedure of 3D animation.

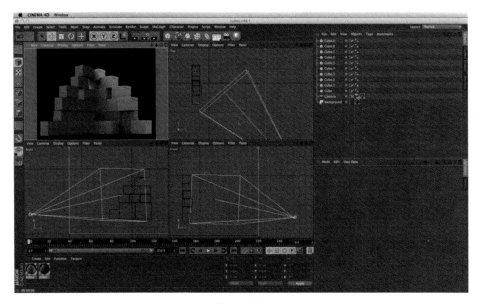

Figure V.15

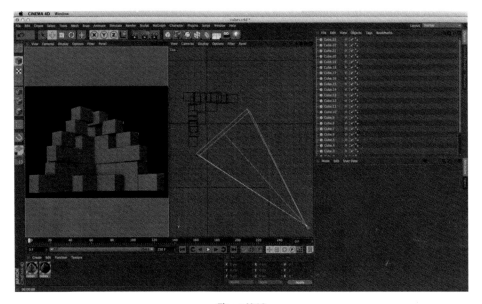

Figure V.16

For illustrative purposes two simple animations will be performed on the scene with which readers can acquire the basic concepts that will allow them to independently study the software more deeply.

5.2 Simulation with lights and animation

The simulation of lights gives depth to the scene. To proceed to the insertion of a light, simply click on the icon shown in figure V.17.

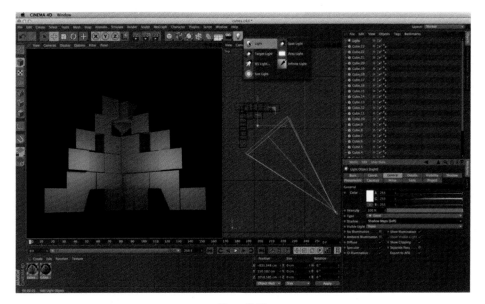

Figure V.17

After adding an omnidirectional light you will need to place it at the center of the scene at about half its height, not forgetting to activate the shadows from the panel **Shadow> Shadow Maps (Soft)**. Once this is done, by starting a rendering you can see the result. Double-clicking on "Light" name the light: **Light_horizontal**.

The principle underlying the animations in Cinema 4D does not differ from that of After Effects. You have to use the key frame, recording the changes by activating the two icons **Record Active Objects** and **Autokeyng** . To animate the light horizontally, previously moved behind the building, place the cursor on the timeline of the key frame at **0** (indicated by the green rectangle) and first click on the icon **Record Active Objects** (in this way you record the first key frame and a small rectangle is shown under the green one) and then after the icon *Autokeyng*. The window which has been used will appear with a red border to indicate that any change to the state of the scene will be recorded.

It should be emphasised that every yellow coloured parameter in the scene can be animated.

Now move the green rectangle on the timeline to frame *250* (corresponding to the tenth second) and then the light to the chosen position. The software will automatically record the other key frame. When the animation is finished, click again on *Autokeyng*.

At this point, to visualise the outcome of the animation to a particular frame, start the rendering or click on the **Play** key for a preview. (figure V.18).

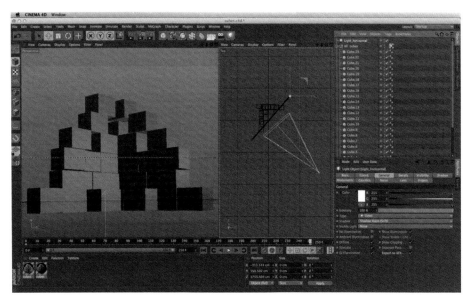

Figure V.18

5.3 Application of textures and effects

Now turn to the application of a material, or texture, on the structure. Select all cubes and, clicking the right mouse button, select **Group Objects**. The group, by default named **Null**, (to be renamed **All cubes**) is used to group together all the elements in a kind of folder.

To apply the texture, you must create the material and to do so you need to go the material command bar, clicking on **Create > New Material** and naming the new material **Cubes** (figure V.19).

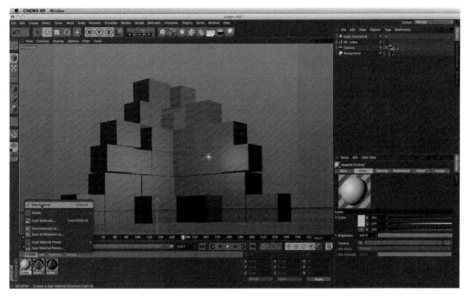

Figure V.19

Having created the new material, a texture can be applied that simulates the desired finish. To do this, click twice on it and, once the reference texture (a common image file) is loaded from the opened window (figure V.20), drag it using drag & drop onto the **All cubes** group.

If you do not change the settings of the default material and you start the rendering of the scene, the result you get, at the 140th frame, is shown in figure V.21.

To make the composition even more interesting, you can insert another effect by going to the modifiers and selecting **Explosion Fx** as in figure V.22.

Also in this case the effect will be applied to the composition only after having dragged it onto the **All cubes** group.

If the globe of the modifier is not centered on the scene, it might seem that no effect has been applied. With the help of the four views, however, it is possible to verify the location and continue to repositioning if necessary.

Leaving the default settings of the effect, it is possible to bring it to life, animating the modifier on the vertical axis, starting from frame 50 and finishing at frame 200. You will achieve a movement of the cubes as the final effect, that after having detached them will return to the original position (figure V.23).

Figure V.20

Figure V.21

Figure V.22

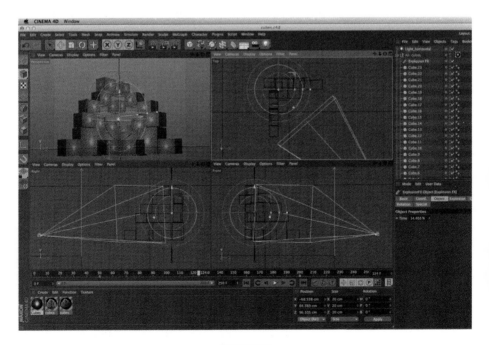

Figure V.23

In figure V.24 the final result is shown at frame 120, including lights and modifiers.

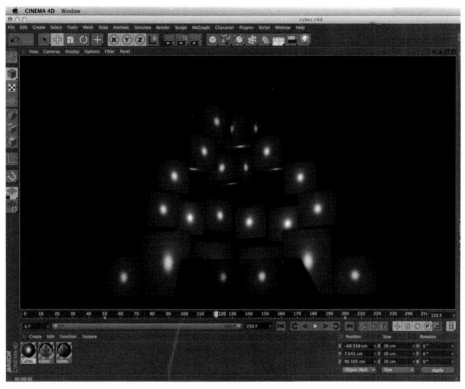

Figure V.24

If you want to be sure of having locked the inserted camera, avoiding possible movements that could affect its exact location, you can activate the relevant function. To do so, click with the right button of the mouse on **Camera > Cinema 4D Tags > Protection** and the related icon will be shown to the right of the camera (figure V.25).

Having achieved the desired result, proceed to the rendering of the scene by clicking on **Render > Edit Render setting** or on the icon 🔲. A window will open like that in figure V.26 from which you can choose the location for saving, the file name (**cubes_3D**), the format and the type of compression through the Options button (choose Photo-JPEG). This done, clicking on OK and leaving unchanged the other options, start the final rendering of the scene by clicking on **Render > Render to Picture Viewer** or on the icon.

With this exercise you have produced the third video which will be added to the files that will be needed to achieve the final composition in Adobe Premiere.

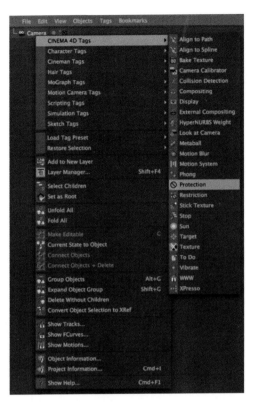

figure V.25

figure V.26

Obviously the effect described is only one of the many that it is possible to create after having set the scene in 3D. The best way to do mapping is to experiment as it is created, because the result of the visual effects on the screen does not always correspond to that projected on the surface and the risk that one runs is that it is less spectacular than intended. Undoubtedly Cinema3D is an excellent instrument for emphasising the shadows and the three dimensionality of the structure and, thanks to the synergy with the plug-in Cineware, that allows the interfacing of files in 3D with After Effects, it is possible to create compositions even more quickly. A well-set scene in cinema 4D represents a very useful support to subsequent compositions used and mixed in Adobe Premiere.

Chapter 6

Audio-video editing:

video mapping in a single file

Where there is much light, the shadow is deeper.

Johann Wolfgang Goethe

El, Video
mapping
performance
competition,
Mapping Lux
Greco, Toledo,
Spain, 2013

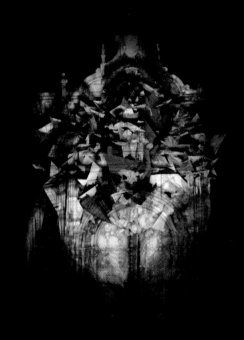

CHAPTER 6

6.1 Design and planning: the Storyboard

Before examining the stages of editing the audio-video, it is appropriate to make a brief reference to some traditional techniques that can be very useful in cases where it is necessary to create animations of a certain duration.

The design stage is critical and represents the moment in which the idea, which will subsequently become a project, is conceived.

During the creation of an animation, a tool is usually used which has become indispensable for many renowned filmmakers: the **Storyboard**.

The storyboard is generally used to represent graphically, in the form of sequences designed in chronological order, shots and scenes that will be created by the animation. It represents a first draft of the graphical display of the final animation. Usually you can note down anything that might assist in creating the scenes, reminders of how make a shot, what effect to apply or the atmosphere you want to create.

A series of storyboards assembled in sequence, with the additions of the audio, represent the **Storyreel**, or rather a video which gives the overall sense of what you intend to re-create.

Before dealing with the topic of "audio-video editing" it is essential to spend a few more words on the storyboard as it enables you to make a reasoned choice of the animations. You can consider it a real tool that enhances the technique of the mapper operator as this will mean that all his skills are directed to the achievement of specific, measurable sequences from the storyboard.

I, Video
mapping
performance
competition,
Mapping Lux
Greco, Toledo,
pain, 2013

Careful study of the architecture on which it will operate is crucial as it allows you to structure the content to fit the design of the facade, so as to let the architectural form communicate with the video content and not the other way round.

Animations that are random and without logical sense are likely to stifle the architecture, unless the final intention is to do just this.

6.2 Open source audio

To create a video mapping performance, an essential element, beyond the visual aspect, is the sound. The concept of the project is mirrored in it and becomes complimentary to the visual element.

Various types of software for the production and manipulation of the sound, like Reason®, Proppelehead® and Ableton®, allow the creation of sounds and allow the creation of sounds and settings to be integrated in the editing stage to the final performance. Certainly those who have no skills in editing music can rely on the support of a variety of resources available online (sounds and loops), which you can arrange and/or modify directly with editing software like Adobe Premiere.

There are various websites from which you can download loops and sounds with the Creative Commons licence. Below are some which can be downloaded in different formats (.mp3, .wave, .aiff etc.):

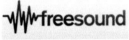

http:/www.freesound.org/

http:/www.soungle.com/

http:/www.pdsounds.org/

The possibility of working with loops and sounds offered under the Creative Commons licence guarantees numerous advantages amongst which:

- the possibility of making a track in macro sections, made up of many individual sounds or loops arranged in the video editing software, so as to have a montage which can be changed at any time depending on the project requirements;
- being for the most part free from rights, requires a simple communication to the author which indicates for what it has been used;
- the huge variety of loops and sounds that can be downloaded allows you to find every type, from loops of drums to guitar riffs, from the sound of breaking glass to the collapse of a wall.

6.3 Adobe Premiere®: assembling and saving an audio-video sequence

Many types of software can be used to create a video mapping project: from those 2D to produce the masks, to those 3D to create virtual models. Obviously everything depends on the mode in which you intend to set up the project.

A stage which cannot be missed out, independently of the choice of working in 2D or 3D, is the final editing, which obviously requires the use of special software.

Working with files produced in software from the Adobe family, equipped as already mentioned in an undisputed interchangeability, the choice necessarily falls on Adobe Premiere®, audio-video editing software based on the timeline.

Assuming you made video sequences in After Effects and Cinema 4D (as seen in the previous chapters), and have downloaded sounds and/or free loops, you can now proceed to the assembly of a small audio-video sequence according to the steps listed below.

Open Premiere and create a new file. In the first panel enter the name of the project (calling it **final assembly mapping**), the location to save the file, and click on **OK** (figure VI.1).

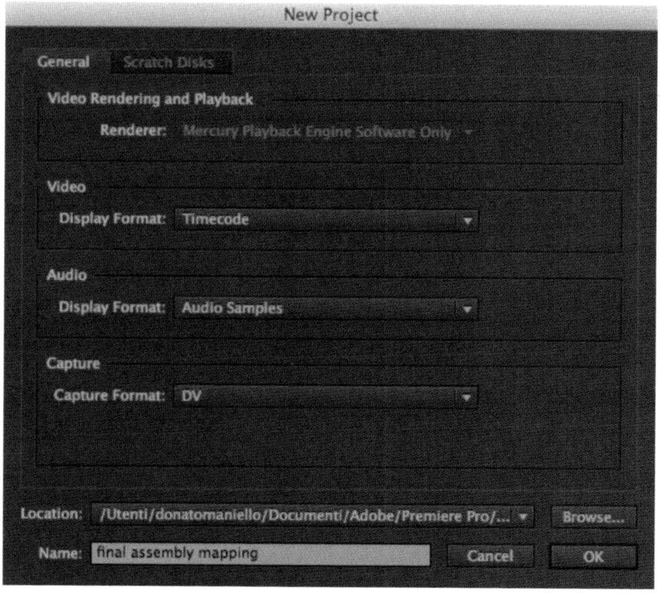

Figure VI.1

A second panel opens with three tabs: **Sequence Presets**, **Settings**, **Tracks**. Given that we must create a file with personalised dimensions and features, do not change the settings of the **Sequence Presets** panel (figure VI.2) and before clicking on the **Settings** tab, give a name to the sequence (**mapping**).

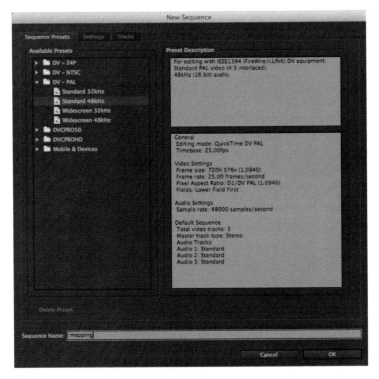

Figure VI.2

The tab **Settings** allows the setting of many essential parameters for the project, detailed below, as shown in figure VI.3.

Editing Mode: *Custom* – This option allows the choice of some editing modes with a series of pre-set characteristics choosing the Personal mode you can activate these characteristics and modify them to your liking.

Time base: *25,00 frames/second* (standard frequency) – the frame frequency (FPS) corresponds to the number of frames per second in the sequence; a higher frequency corresponds to greater fluidity in the video.

Figure VI.3

VIDEO

Frame size: *1024x768 pixel* – The dimensions of the frame refer to the output resolution (in this case the video projector) therefore it should be set on the basis of the dimensions of the clips created before, they too produced according to the resolution of the projector chosen.

Pixel Aspect Ratio: *Square Pixels (1.0)* – This option refers to the the ratio of the sides of the pixel-based standard. To explore this aspect it is recommended that you do an online search on the term Pixel Aspect Ratio.

Fields: *No Fields (Progressive Scan)* – With this option it is possible to choose between two types of image visualisation and transmission: progressive scanning and interlaced scanning.

Display Format: *25 fps Timecode* – This option must be consistent with the "Base Time" option previously set.

AUDIO

You can leave unchanged the base settings.

Sample Rate: *48000 Hz.*

Display Format: *Audio Samples.*

VIDEO PREVIEWS

Preview File Format: *QuickTime (Desktop)* – This option relates to the preview of the sequence and must be consistent with the option "Assmebly mode".

Codec: *Animation* – This option allows the assigning of a codec to the preview of a sequence.

Sequence name: *Mapping* – This option allows the assigning and modification of the name of the sequence that we are going to create.

In **tracks**, you can establish the number of the audio tracks and video with which you will make the composition. Their number can be modified after.

Having finished the setting of these options, by clicking on OK the working interface of Premiere will appear (figure VI.4). The interface can be personalised on the basis of your project's needs; the panels relating to the various tools, of editing and sound management, can be activated from the **Windows** menu shown in the tool bar.

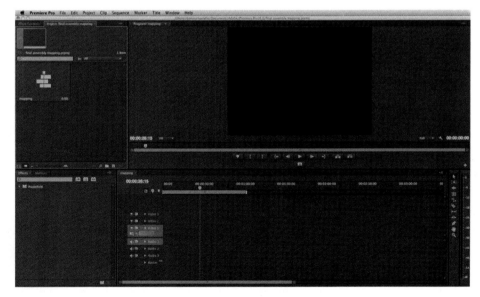

Figure VI.4

Premiere can import numerous types of files, from video to images, from those of sound, to those of Photoshop and Illustrator.

Below the basic tools which are useful to assemble the sequence that you are going to create (figure VI.5).

Figure VI.5

Such instruments, whose use is very intuitive, allow you to carry out the basic actions of editing, such as moving, cutting the clips, the zoom in and the zoom out.

The editing will happen on a timeline, where, by clicking the various clips, you can assemble the final sequence.

For this project, that has the objective of creating a composition through the use of two clips with a fade between them and the incorporated sound, you will need two video files and two audio files.

Premiere has an interface which is very similar to that of After Effects: it has a time bar, offering the possibility to use the labels for visual organisation, effects/transitions, etc.

That decided, start by importing the video files (created in After Effects) and the audio files, previously saved, by clicking on **File > Import**. Automatically the files will be shown as available in the **Project** panel.

Click and drag the two video files (the total duration will be 15 seconds) and the two audio files onto the timeline.

Following this operation Premiere will have placed four tracks, linking each of them in the specific category of reference (audio or video). The levels will be pre-set in a sequential way (figure VI.6).

Create a small assembled sequence, putting in sequence the video and audio clips as in figure VI.7. It will be necessary to cut the clips in order to reduce the replay time or moving the edges or even cutting them with the **Razor Tool**.

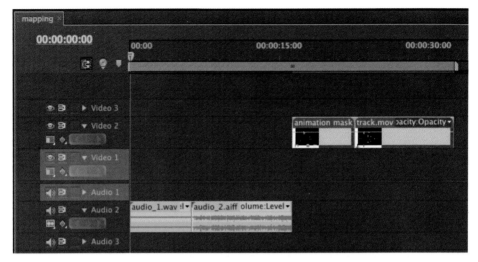

Figure VI.6

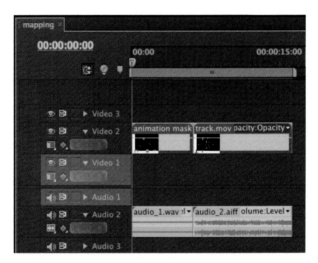

Figure VI.7

Having finished editing the clips, drag the **Cross Dissolve** effect, shown in the **Video Transitions** folder in the **Effects** panel, between the two video clips. The effect will create across fade between the opacities of the clips, which will be shown in the timeline (figure VI.8).

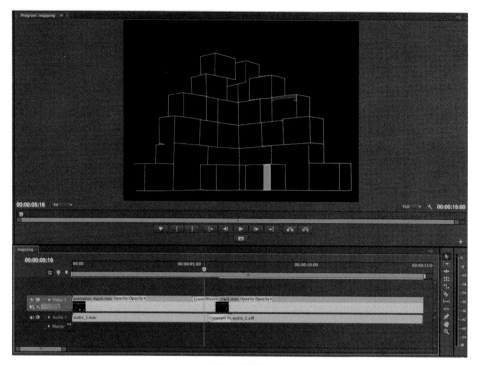

Figure VI.8

Moving on to editing the sound, drag the **Constant Power** effect, shown in the **Audio Transitions** folder in the **Effects** panel, between the two audio clips. The effect, like that of the video, will create a crossfade on the sound, so as to obtain a gradual transition (figure VI.8).

Now select one of the two fade effects carried on the clips (both audio and video) and you will note that in the **Effect Controls** panel, having selected the clip with the effect, you can modify the parameters relating to it.

After finishing the operation of setting the fades, you can continue to exporting the files by clicking on **File > Export > Media …**

During the export stage there will be various tables available with specific options where you can define the setting of the output, for both video and audio.

It is important that the output (the file resulting from the exportation) and the source (the work sequence) have the same parameters, such as size and sound source, using the **Output** window, in **Source scaling**, select **Change Output Size To Match Source** (figure VI.9).

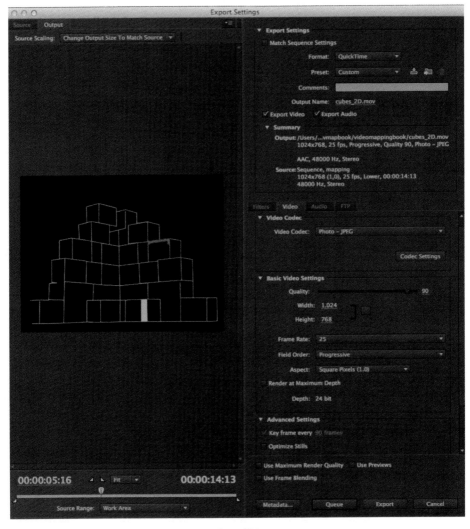

Figure VI.9

In the export stage you will set the most important general parameters as shown below:

Format: *QuickTime* – The format of the video file.

Preset: *Custom* – Allows you to personalise the settings for the resolution of the final video, or to use the pre-set values already available.

Output name – Allows you to choose the name to assign to the files (in this case **cubes_2D.mov**).

Select the options **Export Video** and **Export Audio** to enable the correct export of the video including the sound.

On the tab relating to the **Video** aspects (figure VI.9), you can decide the codec, quality, frame frequency and all the parameters relative to the video.

Modify the video parameters like those below:

Video Codec: *Photo-JPEG* – This option allows you to decide the type of video codec; in this case Photo-JPEG, a video codec used for optimum quality video, but with little compression;

Quality: *90%* – General quality of the video. Obviously check its consistency with the basic options: resolution 1024x768 px and frame rate 25 fps;

Field Order: *Progressive.*

All the values which follow in Video, if selected, will improve the final rendering increasing, however, the runtime.

On the tab relating to the **Audio** aspects (figure VI.10), you can decide the audio codec, frequency and channels.

Modify the audio parameters like those below:

Audio Codec: *AAC* – Allows the setting of the type of audio codec. Choose AAC (Advanced Audio Coding), a compression format created by the MPEG consortium; it provides, for the same compression ratio, superior sound quality to MP3.Channels:

Channels: *Stereo* – You can set the parameter on Stereo if you want to have the Left e Right channels available, or on Mono if you want only one channel.

Having set the output parameters, go on to export the video by clicking on the **Export** button. A new window on the progress bar will allow you to see the progress of the export.

The result of carrying out the exercise will be a montage with two clips associated with two audio clips, in which is applied a fade effect to both the tracks. The final file obtained will have the following characteristics: **resolution 1024 x768 – codec Photo-JPEG – Duration: 00:00:15:00 – Channels: Stereo.**

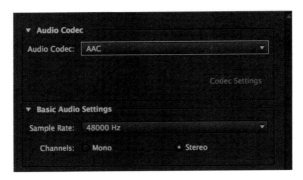

Figure VI.10

You will subsequently convert the video created, calling it **cubes_2d.mov**, using MPEG Streamclip® and you will understand the advantages offered by such software in the conversion to specific formats.

6.4 Transparency: the alpha channel and creating the "external profile"

In the world of digital creativity, one of the fundamental concepts to understand is the use of the channels and their application in the processes of visualising the images. For the representation of the image colours you can use several overlapping channels. The number of channels, the information and the interpolation methods among them, vary according to use that the picture will have, if it will be seen on a monitor or whether it will be printed on a poster.

There are two colour systems of reference to obtain colour information in the images, here described briefly:

Subtractive system (figure VI.11) – This is a system that by combining the three subtractive primaries (Cyan, Magenta and Yellow) with their maximum intensity produces black;

In this system, intended for physical space (printed), there are four channels: Cyan, Yellow, Magenta and Black (CMYK). The Black is shown in the colour system with the letter "K", short for Key to indicate the key colour.

Additive system (figure VI.12) – It is a system in which combining the three additive primary colours (Red, Green and Blue) with their maximum intensity produces white.

In this system, intended for the virtual space (monitor), there are three channels: Red, Green and Blue (RGB).

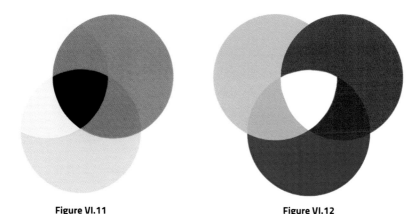

Figure VI.11   **Figure VI.12**

For digital images, the system of reference is additive, due to the RGB colour model, where, as already said, the three channels mixed together with maximum intensity generate white. The alpha channel is an additional channel (not compulsory and not always present), which describes the degree of transparency/opacity of each pixel.

In figure VI.13 the image **cubes_photo.jpg** is shown broken down according to the three channels RGB.

Figure VI.13

The most common image formats incorporating the alpha channel are the TIFF and PNG as regards static images; GIF supports transparency but not the alpha channel.

Regarding the video codecs, the alpha channel is present in some of them, among which the most used is the Animation codec of the QuickTime format or PNG. The alpha channel can be used in all software dedicated to digital processing (Photoshop, Illustrator, After Effect etc.), with different functions in each of them. Generally in an image the alpha channel corresponds to the image itself turned into a black and white version with spot colours.

In Illustrator and Photoshop you can create the alpha channel reproducing, on a new level, the outline of the part of interest (with the Brush or Pen) assigning a black fill to the part you want to hide and puncturing the part you want to show (with a simple operation processing the outline). That done, it will allow you to export a "punctured" image in PNG or TIFF, with the inclusion of transparency or as a punctured mask (figure VI.14).

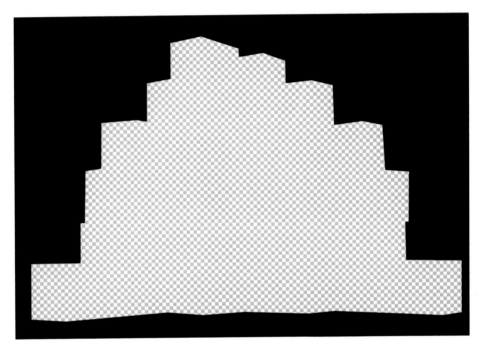

Figure VI.14

The alpha channel can have different uses depending on the software used and the type of project that is to be created. In After Effects or Resolume the alpha channel can be useful to create animations using overlapping layer masks; in Zbrush® (software dedicated to 3D modeling intended for character design) the alpha channel can be useful to create more extruded levels on models like horns or scales; in Illustrator the alpha channel can be used to create layer masks to use as punctured masks.

In video mapping, where the use of various types of software is required in the design phase, the alpha channel is very important and can be used in various ways. In particular, you often use it to create a visual order or to correct any errors, with the creation of a form called external profile. The **external profile** is a layer mask, saved with transparency (therefore including the alpha channel) that allows you to manage the projection area, delimiting it and giving a certain visual order to the projection; it allows you to decide which parts of the structure to delimit or to isolate. Generally, the external profile corresponds to the contour of the projection surface (figure VI.15).

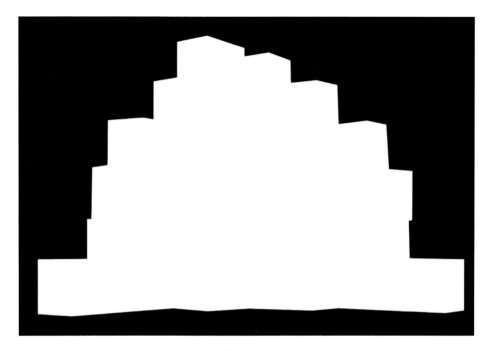

Figure VI.15

Working on the extreme edges of the projection surface may cause problems with the projection, or because of the use of certain effects spreading could be produced or otherwise unwanted results.

The **external profile** is a useful tool for use with precision. To produce it in Photoshop you can trace the outline of the projected surface on the basis of photography in your possession while in Illustrator you could do it by reconstructing layer masks on the same picture, taking care not to go too far into the surface with the tracing, at the risk of cutting some projectable surfaces.

After finishing the outline of the structure, just assign a fill of the colour black to the level that you do not want to show and no fill to the level that you want to show.

In the case of this exercise, the black filling is applied to the wall behind the cubes, while no fill is applied to the level relating to the cubes.

Save the file in PNG (o TIFF) format, renaming it **external profile**.

The **external profile** can be used in the final phase of editing in Premiere (or directly in Resolume) editing it on the appropriate layer that is found by clicking on the timeline on **Video1 > Add Tracks...** (figure VI.16).

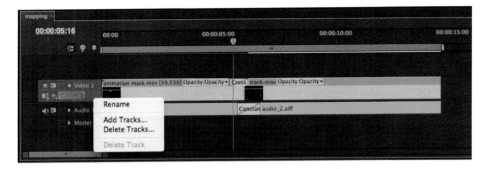

Figure VI.16

Once created, the external profile will need to be imported into Premiere and placed as the first level for the duration of the timeline, so that it influences all levels in the file. At this point you can start the final rendering again as seen in the previous section (figure VI.17).

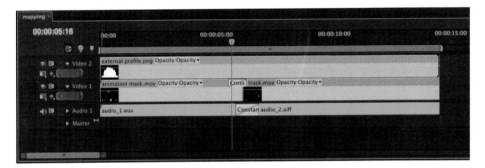

Figure VI.17

6.5 Masks with the alpha channel: "false mapping"

The reconstruction of the layer masks represents a constant for those who create video mapping performances and depending on the design capacity of the user and the type of performance, masks may be used for the most varied purposes.

As mentioned in the first chapter, the technique of "false mapping" requires the use of layer masks with the **alpha channel**, so you can pierced the various parts to show specific video content.

"False mapping" is a very versatile, practical and fast technique, usually used in live/vjset projects or for projects in which the time available to create the performance is less than that which is necessary. With this technique, given a certain reconstruction of the architectural elements, you can show through layer masks video content that will be consistent with the elements rebuilt, without creating the entire *workflow* of the performance (with its concept and storyboard).

In some projects false mapping appears to have a very attractive aesthetic design value. This is especially true in cases of modular structures and in **Stage Mapping**, in which the layer masks are made on a modular basis corresponding to the basic module for the creation of the stage (for example, cubes or tetrahedra).

In these cases the **alpha channel**, like for the **external profile**, will be useful for the selective export of layer masks of the structure.

The technique of **false mapping** can be used in post-production phase (in After Effects or in Premiere) or even directly in Vj software for a live performance.

Returning to the exercise, in the following images we have tried to give a visual reference of the technique of false mapping. By analysing the structure, after an evaluation of the overall shape (figure VI.14) we chose, based on the mapping file, some layer masks (figure VI.18) to be considered for the animation.

Figure VI.18

After choosing the layer masks, export them in PNG format with transparency, so that they can be used to create "holes" that will be crossed with video content.

In figure VI.19 the video projection is shown according to the three layer masks created.

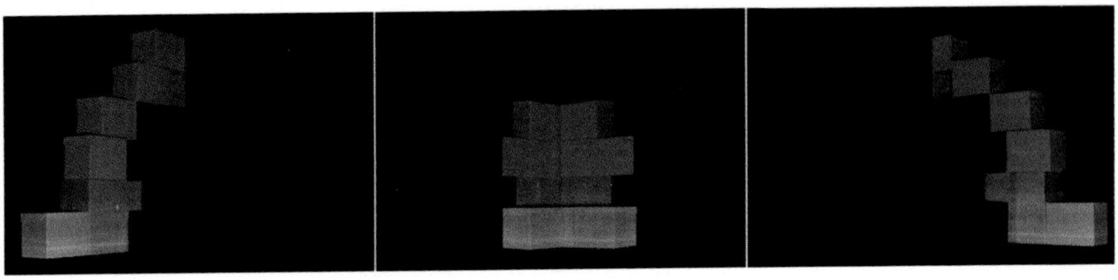

Figure VI.19

At this point you can either continue in Premiere or in After Effects. You simply need to use a video or an image, as in this case, divided into colours (figure VI.20) that has the same file size and position of the mask at the lower level.

Figure VI.20

That done, it will produce a display of only the colour red in the central mask, of blue and red in the mask on the left and red and green in the mask on the right (figure VI.21).

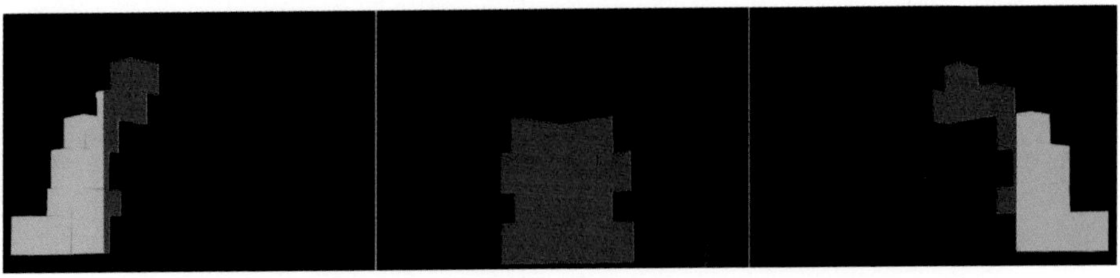

Figure VI.21

If you project the three separate masks on the real model now, the final result will be that in figure VI.22, while if you project them contemporaneously, you will obtain a result like that of figure VI.23.

Figure VI.22

Figure VI.23

The exercise that has been carried out explains in a quick and clear way the concept of false mapping, in that by simply replacing the coloured image with some videos you can give the impression that these perfectly fit the area concerned.

6.6 Converting the various formats: MPEG Streamclip®

Among the many free video convertors available online, one of the best is MPEG Streamclip[14] (available for both Mac and PC).

MPEG Streamclip is a video convertor, as well as a player and editor. You can reproduce and convert many types of films as well as being able to **cut** and **paste** between videos. It allows the conversion of various formats, among which **QuickTime**, **AVI**, **MPEG-4**, **DV**, and it is very useful in that it offers a wide choice of codecs (see chapter 1) giving you complete management of the parameters of conversion.

You may well ask yourself why it is necessary to convert the videos into other formats. In practice it may be because it is necessary to convert a video or read it from another software, or because Premiere does not always export well some formats including DXV. In order to do the conversion correctly you must use a video that is compressed very little, which is why our compositions produced in Premiere and Cinema 4D with the Photo-JPEG codec have been exported. The conversion that makes the most of MPEG Streamclip optimises files for use in Resolume® (which will be discussed in chapter 7).

The DXV Codec, as already illustrated in the first chapter, (owned by the software house Resolume), lets you work with high-resolution video and high frequency frame rate, exploiting the performance of the Graphics Processing Unit (GPU), with minimal use of RAM and CPU.

Another undisputed advantage of the DXV Codec is that it is cross-platform, usable by all the applications that are based on the QuickTime format (MAC e PC); furthermore in the more recent versions, the DXV Codec incorporated the alpha channel as well.

Returning to the conversion in MPEG Streamclip, open the software and click on File> Open File to import the video to convert: **cubes_2D** and **cubes_3D** (you will convert only the **cubes_2D** example). You will notice that it will be displaying the preview of the video that can be played using the video playback controls on the toolbar of the window. Click on **File> Export QuickTime ...** to enter the management panel of the conversion parameters (figure VI.24).

From the management panel you can set all the options of the conversion, from the type of codec to the frame frequency, from the size of the pixels to the adjustment of colour information, so as to obtain a correct export and conversion of the file (figure VI.25).

---

14. http:/www.squared5.com/

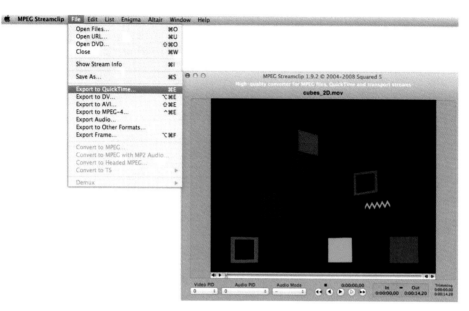

Figure VI.24

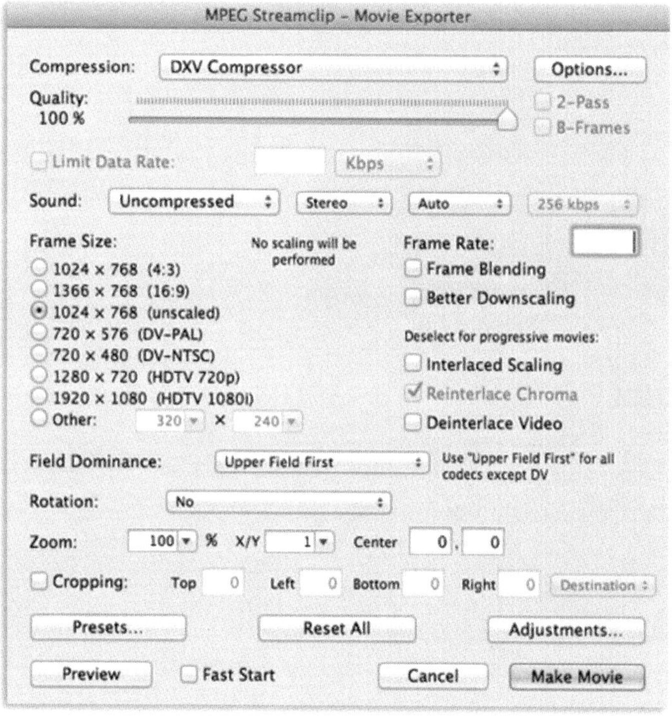

MPEG Streamclip – Movie Exporter

Compression: DXV Compressor   Options...

Quality: 100 %   2–Pass   B–Frames

☐ Limit Data Rate: Kbps

Sound: Uncompressed   Stereo   Auto   256 kbps

Frame Size: No scaling will be performed   Frame Rate:

○ 1024 × 768 (4:3)   ☐ Frame Blending
○ 1366 × 768 (16:9)   ☐ Better Downscaling
◉ 1024 × 768 (unscaled)
○ 720 × 576 (DV–PAL)   Deselect for progressive movies:
○ 720 × 480 (DV–NTSC)
○ 1280 × 720 (HDTV 720p)   ☐ Interlaced Scaling
○ 1920 × 1080 (HDTV 1080i)   ☑ Reinterlace Chroma
○ Other: 320 ▾ × 240 ▾   ☐ Deinterlace Video

Field Dominance: Upper Field First   Use "Upper Field First" for all codecs except DV

Rotation: No

Zoom: 100 ▾ %   X/Y   1 ▾   Center   0 , 0

☐ Cropping: Top 0   Left 0   Bottom 0   Right 0   Destination ▾

Presets...   Reset All   Adjustments...

Preview   ☐ Fast Start   Cancel   Make Movie

Figure VI.25

Depending on the format chosen for the export, you can access the specific submenu of every codec. In the case of the DXV codec, the only option available regards the alpha channel which can be saved or not.

Selecting DXV Compressor, apply the following parameters to the video:

Compression: *DXV Compressor* – The type of video codec for conversion.

Quality: *100%*.

Sound: *Uncompressed - Stereo* – The current audio conversion is optimal, the channels should stereo (Left – Right).

Frame size: *1024x768 px* – The size of the video in conversion phase should be consistent with that of the project.

Frame rate: *25 Fps* – Frame rate consistent with that of the project,

Having done that, click on **Make Movie** to start the conversion of the video. As in After Effects, a Rendering Bar and a preview of the video will be displayed that show simultaneously the progress of the conversion (figure VI.26).

Figure VI.26

It is always better to export from Premiere a .mov file with photo-JPEG compression, with quality varying between 75% and 90% (to have less weight in terms of mb) and export it again with MPEG Streamclip, still in .mov format but with compression DXV at 100%. Proceed to export the file obtained from Cinema 4D® with exactly the same procedure used until now.

The choice of the right codec, based on the projection software that will be used, is of fundamental importance.

The use of a wrong or inappropriate codec could subject the computer to unnecessary overloads due to additional calculations on conversion. That could cause – in the projection phase of the scene in real time – a conspicuous reduction of frames per second with a consequent loss of natural fluidity in the video that could start to jerk. The quality of the animation could be compromised irreparably.

MPEG Streamclip, thanks to the possibility of converting a large quantity of formats, represents a very effective instrument which is useful above all when you need to use videos created by others in which you can disregard the relative codec.

Chapter 7

Resolume Arena®, managing content and warping in real time

If you can dream it, you can do it.

Walt Disney

Video mapping and
sound design
workshop,
Napoli, 2014

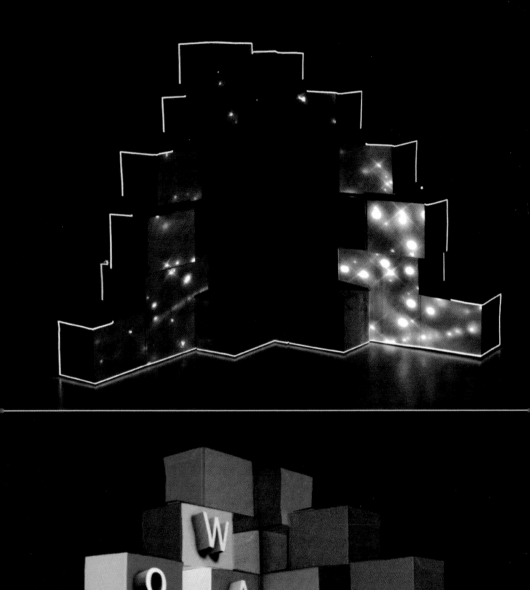

CHAPTER 7

7.1 Resolume Arena and the advanced module of warping

After having created the content (video, audio e pictures) the final phase consists of using some software that enables real time management as well as warping on random surfaces. Resolume Arena®[15], is an audio visual performance tool which lets you play video, audio e audio-visual clips, mix them, apply effects and project the results in a live performance.

Resolume Arena is often used by VJs to mix live video clips so as to create an accompaniment to music, but the best use that it can be used for is audio-visual performances, using the function of BPM (Beats Per Minute) that allows perfect synchronisation of the clips. In addition, the MIDI, DMX and Open Sound Control options make the software especially suitable for shows and interactive installations.

One way to learn to use it is to experiment directly with clips and effects to see the result achieved. Of course, the aim of the book is not to illustrate all the features of the software, which would require a detailed discussion, but some of them will be explored in carrying out the management of the warping and the use of the Advanced Interface will be dealt with.

The more recent releases of Resolume incorporate a module for the distortion of the image - **Image Warping** - and this is what places it among the favourite software for video mapping performances. **Image Warping** is an indispensable tool, as it allows the correction of possible mapping errors resulting from inaccurate construction or caused by small movements of the position of the projector, which would affect the correct model overlap between real and virtual. The use of the warping module directly in Resolume means that you can operate in real time on the structure.

eo
pping and
nd design
kshop,
ɔoli, 2014

---

15. The Resolume Arena software is downloadable as a demonstration version or can be bought on the website at http://www.resolume.com

Returning to the exercise, if the previous stages have been followed correctly, the warping will serve only to perfect the mapping, so as to match the digital playback with reality. By connecting the projector to the computer and opening the software a new composition will be created with a default graphical interface.

Resolume has a very intuitive graphic interface and every panel contains specific functions. The interface will be analysed briefly and is modifiable from the drop-down menu that opens after clicking on **View** in the toolbar from which the view of the various panels can be turned on or off (figure VII.1).

Figure VII.1

Some options are already selected but if you want to work in a generic way, before changing it to suit your needs, it is advisable to use the **Property Panel Layout** that allows the placement of or three panels. **3 Panel** is selected by default. For all phases of this exercise it is recommended to keep the default graphical interface.

By default Resolume has three layers, each of which is made up of nine columns. With the basic configuration it is possible to load up to 27 clips and three Decks, but naturally the number of layers, columns and Decks can be increased at any time according to need.

Below are the main panels which are of greatest use and they are found in Resolume as soon as the program is started:

Composition – Shows the final result relating to the mix of the clips. In essence it shows what will be projected.

Layer – Every clip can be loaded in a layer. It is possible to play one clip at a time and the layers can be combined and overlayed in different ways. To add a new layer go to **Layer > New**.

Clip – This is a video file with or without audio and it shows the base tile on which you work in Resolume. In this panel there are many settings that allow you to modify, move and rotate the clips, play them, pause, stop, and change the audio, etc.

Output monitor – Shows what will be projected, the result of the Composition.

Preview monitor – Allows the preview of a clip other than the one being projected. The preview is visible when you click on the lower part of the clip (shown by its name).

Decks – The clips in a composition are divided into Decks. Passing from one of the Decks to another, the possibilities for changing the scene during the performance increase. To add a new Deck, click on **Deck > New**.

Browser Panel – this panel contains the Files, Compositions, Effects and Sources tabs.

Resolume makes some tools available for the creation of video and various animations which can be activated from the Sources tab on the **Browser Panel**. This tab contains different resources with which it is possible to manipulate and create interesting animations, starting from a full colour or a shade. The effects mentioned are available in the FFGL[16] (Free Frame GL) category.

Once you are familiar with the interface of Resolume, proceed to set the features of the composition by going to **Composition > Settings** (figure VII.2). You need to give a name, a description and the resolution of the composition (Resolume automatically recognises the resolution of the second monitor indicated by **Display 2** – in this case, the video projector) and then click on **Apply**.

---

16. Free Frame GL is a plug-in video dedicated to the generation of video in real time using the power of the OpenGL, specifically designed for programming the field of video. OpenGL, using the power of the graphics card, allows you to manipulate the videos with other resolutions and with a high frame rate frequency. For further information on the language, make an online search using the terms OpenGL or Free Frame GL.

Figure VII.2

In the next section we will compare two methods for overlaying the real model with the virtual one.

7.2 Projection on a real three-dimensional model: the technique of warping to distort the video

Projection on a real three-dimensional model is a more complex type of projection since it must take account of the structure in its entirety. It needs organization and a working method that follows the steps outlined in the previous chapters: the procedure that has resulted in the creation of the file mapping and related videos. When the projection is made on a random surface in 3D, the position and orientation of the projector in front of the surface is of fundamental importance. There exists, as already explained previously, a precise position, a point from which the projected image will seem perfectly aligned; this point coincides with the position of the projector.

To work in a consistent way with the information in your possession it is necessary to set Resolume correctly, so the first thing you have to create is a composition with a resolution of 1024x768 pixels (the resolution of the video projector). Subsequently load on one of the levels, such as layer 3, the image and clips that were created earlier (cubes.jpg, **cubes_2D.mov** and **cubes_3D.mov**) by dragging them with a simple drag & drop from its folder (or by searching through its path from File) and dropping them in the aforementioned level (figure VII.3).

Figure VII.3

The colour map of **cubes.jpg** (as a picture) is vital as it will be used to match the virtual model to the real one. By warping this file, since the video **cubes_2D** and **cubes_3D** were made taking it as a base, they too will be consistently aligned.

To see the clip in the **Output monitor**, simply click on it, while to see it in **Preview monitor** you need to click on the name shown on the clip.

Before projecting the clip, it is advisable to turn on the **Show FPS** function, that allows you to keep the state of the performance under control. Once activated, by clicking on **Output > Show FPS**, you will see the FPS in both the **Preview monitor** and the **Output monitor**. If you play a clip that causes the value of the frames per second to fall below 25 fps, the video will start to go jerky and that means Resolume cannot handle the video efficiently. In order to not undermine the performance, you will need to resolve this problem. The most common cause of a low FPS is due to the codec used (not forgetting that Resolume has its own codec: the DXV). Another cause could be the presence of clips which are too big in terms of resolution, or which have too many effects loaded.

At this point you just have to send the composition to **Display 2** by clicking on **Output> Display 2 (1024x768) - Fullscreen** (figure VII.4).

Figure VII.4

The result displayed, having taken the photo from the same point of view as the video projector positioned on the ground, is shown in figure VII.5.

As shown in the figure, the real model and the virtual one do not match perfectly. This is normal and is due to several factors including the difference in lens between the projector and the camera, and the tilt of the camera when the picture was taken in respect to the axis of the projector lens. These differences are easily resolved in the process of warping. Whenever the difference is significant (figure VII.6), it is appropriate, before working with the commands of warping, to bring the virtual model into the configuration to make it similar as possible to the real model. This can be done by working on the model with the operations of movement, rotation and scaling using the **Transform** panel of the related Layer (figure VII.7).

These operations can be performed in an even simpler and more intuitive way from the advanced panel of the **Output Transformation > Transform**.

This phase of video mapping is the one that uses the principles of geometric transformations (translation along the axes x and y and rotation) and homothety.

Figure VII.5

Figure VII.6

The next step consists of the transition to the advanced stage of warping which starts with the use of **Advanced Screen Setup Output > Advanced** (figure VII.8).

Figure VII.7

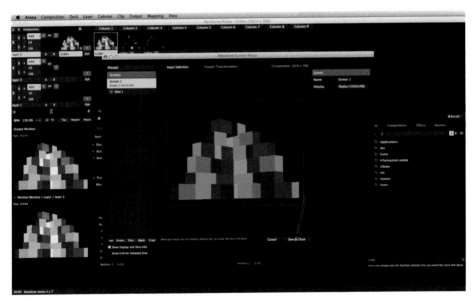

Figure VII.8

The **Advanced Screen Setup** module comprises the following sections:

Screen – Shows the connected devices and the current projection resolution.

Screen 1 – (Display 2 1024 x768).

Slice – contains all the levels of projection that you decide to create. If you want just one level of projection, you only need one slice, and so on. The slice shows the element to which you will apply the warping interventions.

Input Selection – Allows the management of the input video content that will be warped. The enabling of the Input Selection to a particular video means that the dedicated options and the general parameters of Screen or Slice will be displayed.

Output Trasformation – Corresponds to the output video including the changes made in the form of warping. Its activation shows the parameters for the Slice destined to the phase of warping.

First go to the **Input Selection** window, and click on **Slice 1** which is to the left of the screen under **Screens - Screen 1 - Display 2 (1024x768)**. At this point, from **Input Selection**, you can create new Slices depending on the number of layers that you want to insert. Since the videos were shown on one level (layer 3), first select **Slice 1** (left of the screen) and then the source via the **Input source > Layer 3** (figure VII.9). At this point you will see the projected map of colours and, if **Show Display and Slice info** are selected, also Slice 1 and the characteristics of the video card (figure VII.10).

Once the scene is set, you can carry out the warping, distorting first the corners of the composition (homography) and then, as if this was not enough, increase the points of subdivision in the mesh and distort them until the projection matches the real model perfectly (anamorphism). To continue to the transformations, click on **Output Transformation** so as to activate the **Edit Points** function (which manages the homography function) and the T**ransform** function (which manages the homography function) (figure VII.11).

As said before, the first function to use is **Transform** (allows scaling, rotation or movement) so as to centre the colour map on the real scene (in the case shown in the figure the scene has been moved a little higher, by about twenty pixels.

The **Edit Points** function can be used which allows further warping and adjustments (initially the mesh of the colour map has only four corners that can be used as control points and warping). If it is necessary to thicken the mesh you can do so by clicking on **Edit Points > Add Points** (figure VII.12). Through **Output Transformation > Edit Points > Point Mode** it is also possible to choose between three methods to modify the points: **Linear**, **Bezier**, **Perspective**. Of course, the choice of one method over another will depend on the type of modification you wish to achieve.

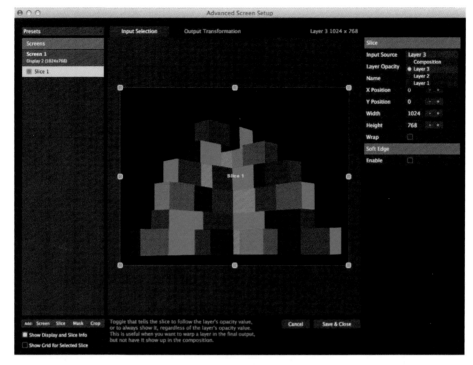

Figure VII.9

Figure VII.10

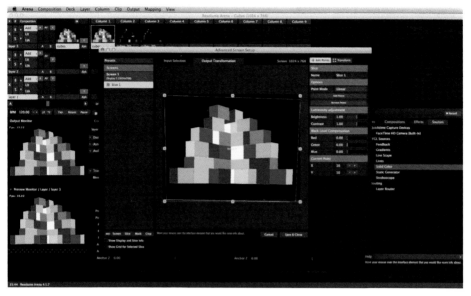

Figure VII.11

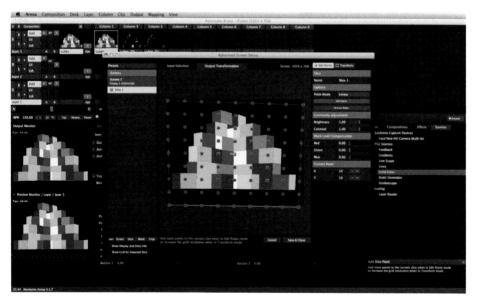

Figure VII.12

It is evident that the thicker the mesh, the more points there will be on which to work and the greater the probability of errors, since there will be points to distort adjacent to the boundary lines of the image (in the case of this exercise the boundary lines coincide with the transition from one colour to another). An excessive thickening might cause errors on other points or even distort the lines that should be straight making them appear angular or rounded.

In these cases experience certainly plays a key role, ensuring that errors of this kind do not occur. Resolume offers the ability to increase or decrease the points of the mesh up to a specified maximum limit. If you want to use less points you can simply use the option **Remove Points**.

Having checked that the mapping is correct, click on **Presets > Save** As to save the file in its present state and call it **CubesWarping**. The process of saving is concluded by clicking on **Save & Close**. You will have saved the warping model of the project, which is modifiable at any time; the ability to change is very useful as more performances can be be repeated on the same structure at different times and so it allows you to greatly reduce the time to dedicated to setup the phases.

In figure VII.13 the points that need to be distorted until the real and virtual models match have been highlighted with white circles.

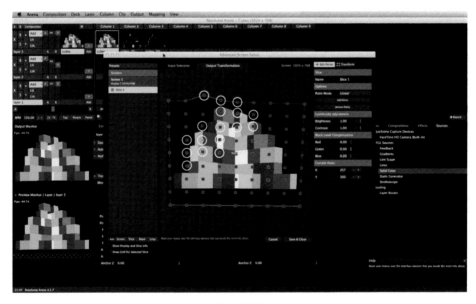

Figure VII.13

To warp the points more easily, it is possible to make use of a grid by clicking at the bottom left on **Show Grid for Selected Slice** (figure VII.14).

In figure VII.15 the various resolutions of grids available are illustrated.

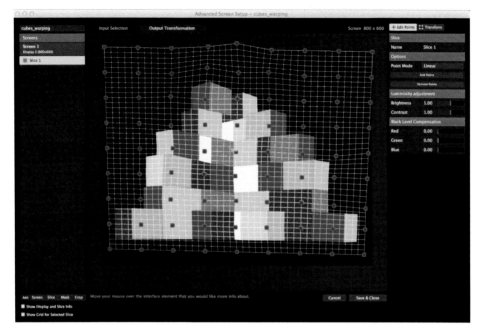

Figure VII.14

Figure VII.15

As shown in figure VII.16, once the warping is completed, the virtual scene will coincide perfectly with the real one and the changes made will be active on the layer and consequently on all videos contained in it. To see the result you only need play the various videos created or the final composition made in Premiere (figures VII.17, VII.18 and VII.19). It is important to note the fact that the photos were taken during the video projection, having placed the camera in a position equal to that of the projector.

Figure VII.16

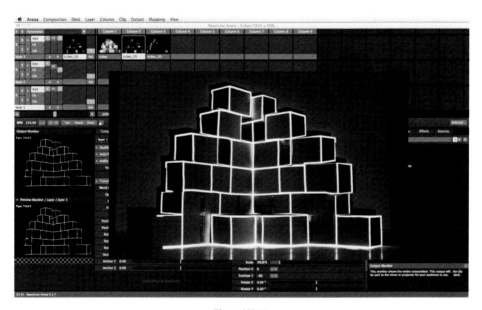

Figure VII.17

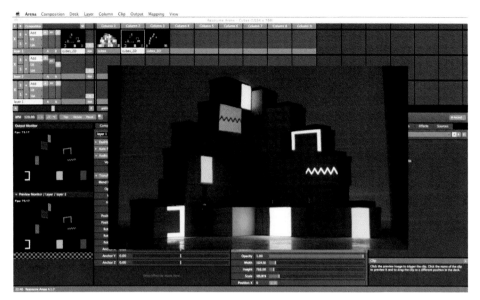

Figure VII.18

Figure VII.19

The automatic playing of the clips may be required; for this Resolume helps as it has a function that automatically puts into play the clips without any operator intervention. To enable this feature you must select the first clip and click **Clip > Autopilot > Play Next Clip**;

you will need to repeat the same operation for the second clip, and so on, while only on the last one click **Play First Clip**. In this way you can set up the separate clips that will be executed in the loop (figure VII.20).

Figure VII.20

7.3 Projection of a real three-dimensional model on surfaces

Projection of a real three-dimensional model on surfaces is the simplest and most widely used type of mapping. This is the case in which the projection is carried out taking into account only the surfaces that make up the structure without considering it in its totality and complexity. In this type of mapping the workflow is dramatically easier and affordable for everyone. The projector can be placed in a random location, although not exactly in front of the area on which you want to project. This type of mapping it is always made via the **Advanced** module – exploiting the knowledge gained in the previous paragraphs – creating more **Slices** and defining the input levels for each of them. To do this you need to move the video files of the example using the drag & drop or the **Browser Panel** following the path **Files> Application > Resolume > Media/Audiovisual** and arrange them on the three default levels (you do not need a particular order of arrangement). Some of the imported videos may not be the same size as the composition (1024x768 px) but rather a different resolution (eg 800x600 px). To adjust the size of the video to that of the composition, just select the clips of interest and click on the option in the parameters panel of the clip (highlighted with the red circle in figure VII.21). In this way, the option will automatically adjust the clip to the size of the composition (figure VII.22). Naturally you will have to repeat the process for each imported clip.

Figure VII.21

Figure VII.22

After the standardisation of the videos to the size of the composition, click on the clip you want to warp; playback will start. Enter the warping module through **Output > Advanced** and, selecting the **Slice** on the **Input Selection** tab, you will notice that in the side panel for the options of the Slices the **Input Source** will be activated (figure VII.23). The **Input Source** option will allow you, after creating a new Slice, to assign a different video content and to define the input signal for the Slice in question. In this way you can make a live mapping with more content, very different from the warping procedure described in the preceding paragraphs in which it was not necessary to create more Slices as there was only one video.

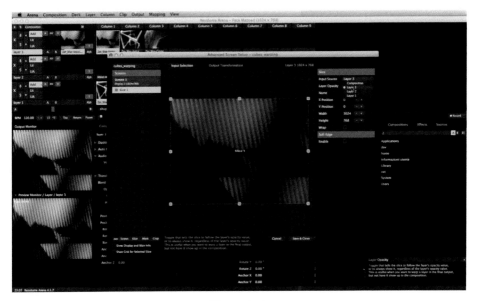

Figure VII.23

The next task is to select **Layer 3** from the **Input Source** and do the warping. To carry out the distortion on the clip you need to keep the Slice selected and click on the **Output Transformation** tab. Given the simplicity of the mapping of the structure in hand, you can drag the grips of the four vertices in the space so that they match with the reference surface (figure VII.24). After the warping of this level, you can create a new Slice and assign different video content from another level, while continuing to keep active the mapping and the playback of the previous clip. This done, you can complete the process by saving the warping you have performed by clicking on **Save & Close** through **Presets > Save**.

Figure VII.24

Extending the same procedure to the other videos, arranged on different layers, the final result is shown in figure VII.25.

Figure VII.25

It is important to always use the grips of the four vertices, and if necessary enable the option **Add Point** to increase the points for warping.

In this section we have explained how to make a real-time mapping, deciding independently the video contents to be allocated to the various projection surfaces. Of course, this type of warping is very useful with simple structures, stage mapping or live mapping, but you cannot use it if you want to take full advantage of the architectural appearance of a building or a monument. In such cases, in fact, due to the lack of a reconstruction of the layer masks it is impossible to create content based on the structural elements of the architecture.

7.4 Creating a mapping reference with the technique of warping

As mentioned above, using the advanced options of Resolume, you can easily pre-warp the image to be projected to compensate for possible distortions. In this way you will always have a correctly projected image on a flat surface, regardless of the projection, the orientation and the lens of the video projector. Essentially a clip must be loaded in Resolume for each face that you want to map and warp the related videos and/or images through the use of the Advanced Interface.

In the following example ten levels are used and a **Solid Colour** is loaded on each level through **Sources** (figure VII.26) on the **Browser Panel** (of course, as an alternative to **Solid Colour** videos or images could be used). The default fill colour of **Solid Colour** is red, and bringing the saturation to a value of zero will produce the colour white.

Figure VII.26

Load a **Solid Colour** on each level and, activating the panel for the advanced options as shown before, you can warp the related **Slices** (whose number will match with that of the layers) on the faces of the cubes (figure VII.27).

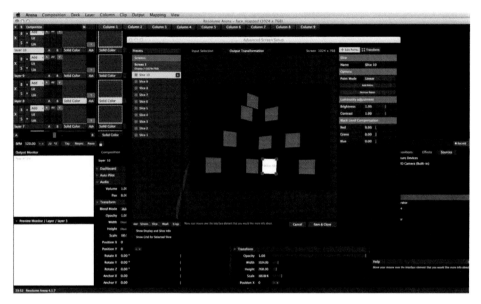

Figure VII.27

The result achieved is that shown in figure VII.28.

Figure VII.28

The method described allows you to map surfaces located arbitrarily in space with extreme simplicity and speed. By mapping the structure completely, through **Solid Colour or** different colours (for example, to differentiate between the faces), you can use the result as a real file of final mapping. Basically you will obtain a result similar to what you will see using Photoshop with the method of the mapping tracing (see Chapter 9).

To extract the file, which will be saved on the path **HD (Hard Disk) > Documents > Resolume Arena> Recorded**, you have to click on **Output > Snapshot**. The file will have the size set for the document, in this specific case 1024x768 px (figure VII.29).

Figure VII.29

In the mapping file obtained you can carry out all the tasks of creating 2D e 3D video shown in the previous chapters.

The procedure described allows you to minimize the adjustments made during the warping phase as it is as if you had taken a "snapshot" from the same point where the projector is placed and with the same lens, so the virtual model and the real one always match.

In this chapter we have seen how to edit a single file using the warping module, so as to have a single surface of warped projection. By analysing an example of live mapping we have discussed the procedure with which to create more projection surfaces with different video content and to create some visual references for the mapping. This has highlighted the potential of the warping technique, the multiple uses depending on the user's design capabilities and therefore the indispensability of the tool of video mapping.

Chapter 8

Surveying architecture: the first step to video mapping outdoors

There is a role and function for beauty in our time.

Tadao Ando

Click Scanner,
Video mapping
performance, Church
of S. Maria della Luce
Mattinata (FG), 2013

CHAPTER 8

8.1 The architectural survey

What has been seen so far has served to learn the basic techniques that allow you to make a subsequent more complete step in creating video mapping on more complex surfaces. The transition from mapping of a scaled structure indoors to the mapping of architecture poses additional problems related to the change of dimensions, such as the need to evaluate in a much more careful way the power of the video projector, its location and the type of lens.

The architectural survey, when working outdoors is the starting point for creating the mapping files that allow you to work on outlines, layer masks, 3D model and animation. The difference from the procedure described above lies in the different management of the original files that require a different process to ensure that the virtual model and the real match almost perfectly.

The **architectural survey** will serve to collect the necessary and sufficient information to permit the reconstruction of the facade and can be briefly divided in two phases: the retrieval and the rendering.

The retrieval is the phase in which measurements are collected and they can be:

- **direct**: when the article is measured manually, using a tape measure, a metric wheel or laser rangefinder;

- **photogrammetry**: when the article is photographed and the photograph is rectified with suitable devices;

- **digital**: when a 3D laser scanner is used;

The **rendering**, on the other hand, is the phase in which all the information collected is used to graphically reproduce the building. Today, with the arrival of digital techniques of representation, it is possible to talk about modelling, thanks to which you can have a three-dimensional model from which to obtain representations of all the planes such as elevations and/or sections. Thanks to 3D laser scanner technology, even if not of a professional type, the building can be measured with a good approximation.

:k Scanner,
leo mapping
formance,
urch of S.
ria della Luce
ttinata (FG),
13

Different types of "mapping" will arise according to the methods of retrieval and rendering used.

8.2 Measuring the building: which measurements are really necessary?

Carrying out a full architectural survey is a good starting point for the creation of a video mapping event. Usually the measurement of the base and the height of the building are sufficient, through which you can obtain all other necessary measurements.

Before proceeding to the survey of an architectural structure, it is advisable to check if there is one already available at some local authority, or technical office, that has carried out work on it. However, it often happens, especially for ancient structures, that the surveys available are digital scans of old projects and do not carry any measurement; in this case the plan is almost useless.

Of course, it is possible to determine the scale of the plan and all the necessary information, even if the measurements are not present.

For example, if you had a plan on which the metric scale is not shown and you want to determine the scale of image, it is sufficient to note, in situ, an actual measurement of the building (value A – in centimetres) and check on the plan available as to how many centimetres this corresponds (value B). The scale of the plan can be calculated with the by the simple equation $S = A / B$.

Once the scale of the image on the plan is established, simply measure with a ruler the element of interest on the plan and multiply the value obtained by the scale factor S, thereby obtaining the actual measurement of the element expressed in centimetres.

The use of existing surveys can be useful, even if experience on the ground has shown us that they are best used only for approximate measurements (often they are inaccurate or not updated with the various tasks that have affected the structure over the years).

The recommended solution is to reconstruct the elevation based on a photo after having "rectified" the picture by removing the optical irregularities caused by the lens, making sure to take it from the point of view of the projector. For the survey it is necessary to have a metric wheel or a laser rangefinder that could also be useful to calculate the height of the building.

Once the base and height of the building is known, you also know how big is the "screen" on which to project. This allows you to evaluate what type of projector and which lenses to use. It is obvious that the measurement of the base of the building can be calculated simply and directly while the calculation of the height is a little more complex. In this regard you can choose one of the procedures that will be explained in the following paragraph which use simple notions of trigonometry and a scientific calculator.

Assuming that you have a plan which is to scale, simply, as mentioned above, measure the height on the drawing with a ruler and multiply by the scaling factor (for example, if on a plan of scale 1:100 the height of the building is 15 cm, in reality the building is 15x100 = 1500 cm or 15 m high).

It is certainly useful to have as many measurements as possible identified in a direct manner (height of windows and doors, the distance between one balcony and another, or between one window and another) as it may be useful in the process of rectifying that photo so that the photo meets the right proportions between the elements.

You should record these measurements directly on the paper on which you sketch the facade; having the measurements shown on the sketch of the elevation will be very useful once back in the office.

8.3 Calculating the height of a building

To calculate the height of a building with a laser rangefinder, simple follow the procedure below. Position the laser rangefinder on a tripod at point A at a specific height **hc** from ground level (figure VIII.1). with the laser rangefinder measure the distances **AB** and **AC**; knowing the height hc you can apply Pythagoras's theorem to obtain the height of the building **ht**.

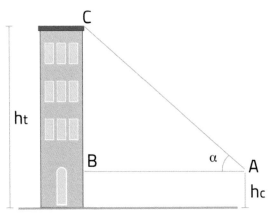

Figure VIII.1

$$ht = CB + hc = \sqrt{(AC^2 - AB^2)} + hc$$

Another way to calculate the height of the building is using a homemade sextant (figure VIII.2). The sextant, positioned in the same way as the rangefinder allows you to calculate the angle **α** between the horizontal plane and the highest point of the building. Having available the angle **α**, the distance **AB** and **hc**, it is possible to calculate **ht**.

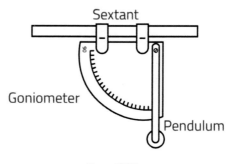

Figure VIII.2

$$ht = AB*tang(α) + hc$$

For example
  AB = d = 15 m; α= 36°; hc = 1,7 m
  ht = b*tang(α) + hc = 15*tang(36) + 1,7 = 12,59 m

Of course, in the two previous cases, it was assumed that rangefinder and the base of the building were placed at the same level. Otherwise you would have to add or subtract the difference in height between the two elements.
As an alternative to the methods described, one of the many Apps for Smartphones can be used that use the same principles of trigonometry.

8.4 The right video projector

In choosing a video projector the features to bear in mind are essentially three: **Ansi Lumens**, **Throw ratio** and **Resolution/Aspect ratio**.

Ansi Lumens

The value of Ansi Lumens depends on three factors: the overall brightness of the place in which the performance of video mapping will take place, the size of the facade and, in theory, also from the "gain rate" of the screen. For proper evaluation you should use a lux metre (figure VIII.3) but the measurement should be made under the same lighting conditions in which you are going to do the performance.

Figure VIII.3

This means that the conditions of darkness in which you will operate should be recreated; for a faithful measurement permission to turn off the public lighting should be requested (see chapter 10), as it will be on the evening of the mapping.
In the following table are shown the principal values of illumination in relation to the common conditions of lighting.

Illumination	Conditions of lighting
100.000 lux	Strong sunlight
10.000 lux	Full daylight
500 lux	Office lighting
80 lux	Low level lighting
1 lux	Moonlight

As an alternative to measuring with a lux metre, another method for selecting the Ansi Lumens of the projector, the result of experience in the field with gloWArp, is the use of a simple empirical formula in optimal dark conditions. This formula, although slightly overestimating the final value, allows you to evaluate the approximate but sufficiently correct, Ansi Lumens necessary, remaining within a certain range of safety.

Before introducing the formula cited above it is essential to mention an important feature of the screen/ projection surface. This feature is the Gain Rate, which indicates the ratio between the amount of light shining on the surface of the screen and how much of it is then sent back in the direction from which the light itself came. The common projection screens reflect the light projected almost like a mirror.

In a similar way to projection screens, you can divide the projection surface depending on the dominant colour.

Surfaces can be divided as:

- very dark: gain < 1

- light: gain = 1

- very light: gain > 1

For video mapping performances it is difficult to assess the gain with the right approximation, except in particular cases in which the colour of the facade is particularly dark or particularly light. Usually you assume it to be equal to 1, so considering the unit value it will not affect the formula we developed for the empirical calculation of Ansi Lumens (AL).

Knowing the area of the projection surface **A** (value expressed in square metres) and the value of the gain rate, after setting a multiplication coefficient **K** always equal to 40 and defining the parasite **Y** as the amount of illumination you have:

$$AL = (A *K) / gain + Y(1,2,3)$$

As for the illumination parasite Y, according to the lighting conditions at the boundary, you can choose between the values shown in the following diagram:

Y1 = 1000/2000 AL	illumination parasite absent or poor
Y2 = 3000/4000 AL	illumination poor or averagely present
Y3 = 5000/6000 AL	illumination poor or averagely or highly present

To further clarify what is shown the practical procedures to be followed in a specific situation are detailed. First, during the technical inspection you will find:

1) the height of the building **h** (height of the "screen")

2) the width of the building **b** (width of the "screen");

3) the distance at which to position the video projector **d**;

The ratio **h/b** allows you to assess the **Aspect Ratio**, which includes the performance, while the ratio **d/b** determines which lens to use and so the **Throw ratio**.

For example, given the following values of **b, h, d, Y** and **gain** rate:
  b = width of building = 20 m
  h = height of building = 18 m
  d = distance at which to position the video projector = 15 m
  gain = 1
  Y= Y2 = 3000 AL

the Ansi Lumens required can be calculated as:

$$AL = (20*18*40) /1 + 3000 = \textbf{17400 Ansi Lumen}$$

From the calculation it appears that it would require a projector of 17,000 AL. Certainly it could also be a projector with a slightly lower brightness, but for peace of mind you could also choose a projector of 20,000 AL. Obviously a different value of Ansi Lumens implies a different hiring cost, so the evaluation should be made keeping in mind this aspect of no small importance.

Throw ratio

After calculating the Ansi Lumens, the Throw ratio can be calculated:

$$\textbf{Throw ratio} = \textbf{d/b} = 15/20 = 0.75$$

Having obtained the value of the Throw ratio you should verify on the technical sheet the reference value of the lens of the video projector. The lens value of 0.75 does not exist, so you will have to take one that is as close as possible to 0.8 (wide angle lens).

It is important to remember that the wide angled lens are fixed and do not allow zoom, while the variable lens usually have such a feature. Furthermore, some video projectors can memorise the zoom settings which can be very useful if the zoom has already been adjusted on one occasion and you want to use the projector in the same position at a later date; in this case simply select the required zoom from the memory.

Resolution/Aspect ratio

Resolution and aspect ratio are two related factors and essentially depend on the dimensions of the facade. Knowing the dimensions of the facade, it is appropriate to think in terms of proportions, as this results from the various units of measurement. Taking pictures of the building, when you work on it you will think in pixels% and not in metres and centimetres.

In the case of our example we have:

$$\textbf{Aspect ratio = b/h} = 20/18 = 1,1 \text{ recurring}$$

Comparing this aspect ratio value with those available, it is clear that in the format 4/3=1,3 recurring, it will include this image in that it results as 1,1 < 1,3. Therefore you will work in the format 4/3 and at one of the resolutions available for such aspect ratio.

Usually all projector manufacturers provide software that allows you to calculate, depending of the lens and distance, the values needed to define the size of the projection. Alternatively, these values can be found in the sites that have been shown in the links in section II of chapter 3.

In conclusion, once the brightness, the distances, the lenses, etc. has been evaluated, the features of the video projectors that would be needed in the given example are the following:

Brightness: 17.000 AL

Resolution: XGA – 1024x768 px

Aspect ratio: 4:3

Lens: 0.8 fixed

Video projector height

Having determined the height, you can choose the right scaffolding to support the projector, the appropriate fasteners and a security plan that must be made by qualified personnel if the projector is placed at a height greater than 2 metres.

As for the height of the projector it is important to bear in mind that it depends on the place and space chosen. The majority of video projectors have central projection, so the optimal height for positioning it is at about half the height of the building. When using a lens that is not fixed you can place the projector lower down, compared to the building, and recalibrate everything thanks to the lens shift function, which, however, increases the optical distortions.

Positioning it lower down, however, could lead to large distortions, such that the projected image is not contained within the facade. In these cases it could be corrected by distancing the projector from the projection surface or, where possible, by changing the lens. As a last resort you could also think about linking together several projectors using the blending mode technique through a suitable external video card.

The choice of projector requires a technical site visit and the assessment of the maximum brightness which is present. Usually most of the ambient light (stray light) is due to street lamps and illuminated signs that could be in the vicinity.

Sometimes it happens that, although being granted permission to turn off public lighting, not all are turned off. In such cases, you can find yourself in the presence of a lot of stray light that could disrupt the projection, especially in the case in which the video projector does not have the right brightness. In that situation, not being sure of the darkness that can be achieved, it is appropriate, if the budget allows, to overestimate the brightness of the projector. Definitely a "guarantee" may be to use a projector with a brightness of at least 10000/12000 AL.

Naturally, the greater brightness of the projector will not create dark, but in the phase of projection the high brightness of the video projected will reduce the visibility of the background architecture that you would see as a result of present stray light. If you do not have budget limits you can avoid the above considerations and overestimate from the outset the system regardless of lighting conditions and the size of projection.

8.5 Positioning the video projector and the spectator's point of view

Once the features of the projector have been defined, you need to determine its location. The basic rule of video mapping assumes that you have taken a photograph from the point of view of where you intend to place the projector and to check in principle the performance from the same point of view. Fortunately the boundaries in which you are operating are wide and allow you to make some mistakes as long as falling within certain limits.

To understand the importance of the position of the video projector and of the correct display (anamorphism) some text was projected on the cubes. The text results correctly displayed in figure VIII.4 in that the point of view from which the photo was taken matches with the point of view of the projector (from which all the mapping files were obtained). Taking another photo from a point of view that does not match the correct one, the result shown in figure VIII.5 is obtained in which the text does not follow the same perspective of the cubes and appears distorted and without any relation to it. In fact, when projecting onto a random 3D surface there is only one point at which the projected image will seem perfectly aligned and that point coincides with the position of the projector. In the case of figure VIII.4 the projector was placed properly (in the same position from which the picture was taken) and it is clear that everything matches perfectly including the text which follows the same perspective as the cubes.

Figure VIII.4

Figure VIII.5

Usually it is possible to locate the video projector a few metres away (either higher or lower) in respect to the view of the spectator without altering the overall view of the effects, provided that they comply with the previous rule that that the projector placement matches the one from which the photo was taken.

Imagine placing the projector at the point of view of the spectator which, not being unique, would not be an advantageous point of view. The above is the same situation that occurs at the cinema where the projector is placed metres higher than the central rows of the audience but no director would imagine even remotely making the film bearing in mind the point of view of all the spectators.

Naturally, it is the task of the performer to evaluate when a photograph is necessary and when not, or rather it is necessary to respect the basic rule and when it is possible to put it aside, in the case that, for example, the spectator is far below or above the point in which the video projector is positioned.

Imagine, absurdly, a building 50 metres high, on which videos will be projected from the altitude of 20 metres and that the projector is positioned at 35 metres high. In this condition, it would be important to consider the position of the spectator and the animations should be created considering this particular aspect.

Of course, this hypothesis is an extreme case and it should be considered whether it is possible to position the video projector lower down in respect of the surface, making use of the lens shift function.

The photograph may not be necessary, however, if you place the projector at a distance such that we could consider, very approximately, its point of view coinciding with infinity (in the same way that happens in the orthogonal projections). In this case an architectural survey of the elevation could be used, after verifying that the .dwg file (extension of files generated in Autodesk Autocad®) does not contain anomalies due to incorrect graphic rendering.

That said a case in which the basic rule was not respected can be analysed to see what happened during projection. Figure VIII.6 shows a photograph taken on the occasion of the Next Step Festival 2012 - Milan, the Festival where gloWArp was selected with the performance entitled Butterflight effect.

Figure VIII.6 – Next step Fetival 2012, Chiostro dei Glicini, Milan (gloWArp performance).

It is clear that the projection on the arches does not match perfectly with the architecture and creates white "crescent moons". To correct this error the technicians have distorted the video with "warping" but with the result of changing the overall appearance. It is a known fact that the white lines are not vertical but visibly distorted. This case is very interesting, in that not having respected the basic rule, it was enough to place the projector at about 3 feet above the spectator (the projector was placed behind one of the central windows, the same as those in the photo in question) to generate the problem. The photograph was in fact taken from the point of view of the spectator on the ground floor and then the 3D model, layer masks, and all mapping files were made replicating this error.

The wrong position also generates an error with the shadow that is formed under the vaults due to the projection coming from above. The error could have been avoided either by respecting the basic rule or by placing the projector lower down, so as not to create unsightly shadows on the projection.

A different situation, relating to a successful event, is the example in figure VIII.7, at the GLOWFestival 2013 (www.glowfestival.it)[17]. From the picture it is clear, even though the surface is more extensive and complex, that simply respecting the basic rule has achieved a perfect fit between the surface and the projected video.

In short we can say that if you do not respect the basic rule mapping may be irretrievable since the final stage of warping only corrects optical distortions but does not correct the views or, even less, reconstruct it giving rise to a new perspective.

Figure VIII.7 – GLOWFestival 2013, Palazzo di Città, Ostuni (BR).

17. Event curated by the gloWArp studio and the Associazione Primitivi Digitali.

Chapter 9

Methods for mapping a surface

Architecture is nothing more than order,
arrangement, beautiful appearance, the proportion of
the parts to each other, convenience and distribution.

Michelangelo Buonarroti

Remains, Video mapping
performance,
Archaeological remains
Lombard period –
Galleria Malies,
Benevento, 2013

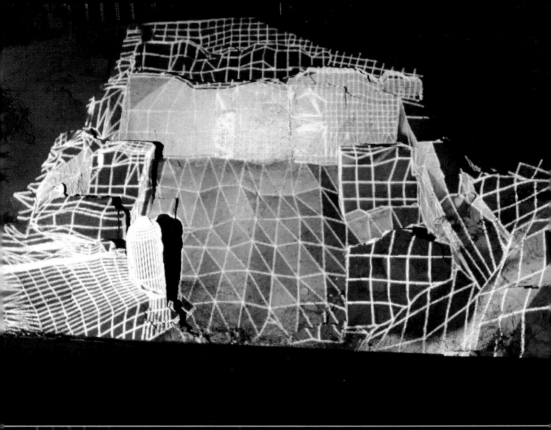

CHAPTER 9

9.1 Comparison of methods

The mapping of a surface can be carried out in various ways and, having experimented with different types during our professional activity, we can affirm that it is appropriate to choose from time to time that which works best in the location, in the time available and according to the complexity of the surface. Depending on the method used, the workflow changes even if the final objective, the creation of a mapping file, does not change.

The methods available today are:

- **Trace mapping**: existing real scenes;

- **Photographic mapping**: existing real scenes;

- **Mapping with 2D scanning**: existing real scenes;

- **Mapping with 3D scanning**: existing real scenes;

- **Virtual mapping**: real scenes not yet existing but planned in 3D.

In the current chapter only trace mapping and photographic mapping will be examined, leaving to volume 2, to be published later, the discussion of the other methods.

9.2 Trace mapping

Remains,
Video mapping
performance,
Archaeological
remains
Lombard
period –
Galleria Malies,
Benevento,
2013

Trace mapping is the simplest type of mapping and plans, with the resolution of the projector known, the use of Photoshop for tracing in real time the forms of a building. It turns out to be a very fast method if the facade is particularly simple, but does not take into account the photographic texture as those that will be produced will only be colour maps, or masks, for each element of the facade. This

211

method is very useful when, using 2D scanning, part of the scene cannot be fully included in the work area. In fact, with this method we can trace the missing parts (refer to Volume 2 for further discussion).

With trace mapping very few adjustments are needed in the process of warping as having "taken the picture" with the same projector lens and from the same point of view, the virtual model and the real always coincide. We do not recommend trace mapping in the case of very large and complex surfaces, both in terms of the time required for tracing the facade (which is much easier said than done) and due to the movement of the work area in Photoshop, which requires closing and reopening the file again to work on it when approaching the edges of the sheet (the area that cannot be locked). The latter problem is solved with the use of Gimp, open source software similar to Photoshop, in which this difficulty does not occur.

Having obtained the mapping file for the colour map it is then possible to overlap it with the real photo and distort it until they match so that you can then use the photograph as a texture for the model in 3D.

To make a draft map, you need to have the projector with its related lens, but it is not necessary to know the height at which it will be placed as it is sufficient that the whole façade is illuminated by its light beam.

In this case the position of the video projector has a secondary role and is only considered according to the space and to the progress of the event in safety. The gloWArp studio used it for some of its early works including the video mapping in the inner court of the City of Minervino Murge (BT) and the one on the facade of the Church of San Gerardo Maiella di Calvi (BN).

Taking as reference the case of video mapping on the facade of the church of San Gerardo Maiella di Calvi, the phases of the work carried out are listed below:

1) choice of the type of mapping: tracing, given the simplicity of the facade;

2) choice of video projector: Ansi Lumen, lens, XGA resolution;

3) choice of the position of the video projector: until all the surface is illuminated by the video projector.

It is useful to know the keyboard shortcuts listed below (valid for both Mac and Pc replacing **cmd** with the command **ctrl**) as this will avoid passing the mouse from the second monitor (projection projector) to that of your computer (first monitor). It can happen that on large surfaces you lose the reference of the mouse pointer, dramatically increasing the time required to conclude the operation. Instead using keyboard commands, while remaining on the second monitor to work, the problem does not arise (figure IX.1).

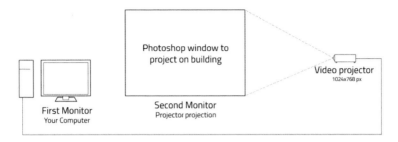

Figure IX.1

At this point you work in Photoshop as described below:

Create a document of the same size as the output of the projector (1024x768 px and 72 dpi - second working monitor) by going to **File > New** (figure IX.2). Set the zoom to 100% (by changing the percentage value shown on the bottom left) and move the document onto the second monitor by dragging the work window to the right or left of your desktop, depending on the setting options. Finally, remove the rulers, if visible, going to **Views> Rules** or by pressing the "**F**" key until you see only the document.

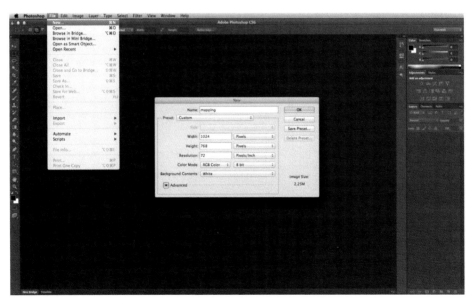

Figure IX.2

Create a new layer, **shift+cmd/ctrl+n**, for each item that you want to map and trace it using the **Pen tool** [pen icon]. After closing the shape, click the "**A**" key and select the created item (it activates the grip at the top), **right click> create vector mask**. Select in the Layers palette either the **Layer Thumbnail** or **Vector Mask Thumbnail** (linked together by a chain icon), choose the colour clicking on **Set foreground colour** in the **Tools** palette. Pressing "**G**" from the keyboard or by selecting the **Paint Bucket Tool** from the **Tools** palette, colour the shape.

You can make any adjustments by pressing A on the keyboard and going to edit the vertices of the shape created until this coincides with the element chosen. You can add or remove any points by entering the submenu of the **Pen tool** and selecting either the **Add Anchor Point tool** or the **Delete Anchor Point Tool**.

Finally, it is expedient to save the various paths by accessing the relevant menu, double-clicking on the **Path**, to which you can give a name and save it. You will need to do this for each new form because it does not save automatically. The procedure must be repeated for all elements of the facade. The procedure is quite long and the execution time will depend on both your experience of using Photoshop and your skills of managing a monitor which is out of scale.

Save the file with the extension **.psd**. The procedure for saving the **Paths** allows you to export the file to Illustrator going to **File > Export > Paths to Illustrator**. At this point you can select all the shapes or only those that you are interested in. When you open the files in Illustrator the **Convert to Artboards** window will appear. You only need to select **Crop Area(s)** to be sure of working in the same resolution (figure IX.3).

Figure IX.3

The result achieved, after about three hours of work, is that shown in figure IX.4.

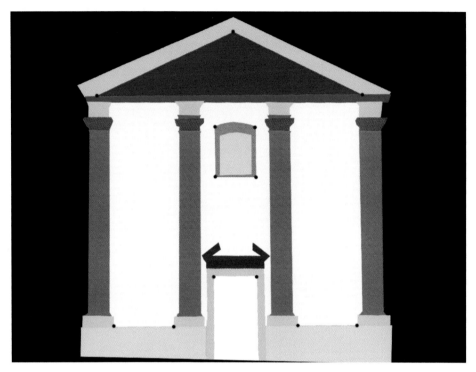

Figure IX.4

The file has been cleaned up from blemishes and errors caused by tracing in real time, which is subject to little precision in defining the contours because of the very large scale of the work.

The black circles visible in figure, useful but not necessary, serve as a reference to centre perfectly the video projection on the facade before the start of the show. The final result achieved by projecting on the architecture is shown in figure IX.5.

The interesting aspect of this method is that, after taking note of the position of the projector, even after some time, you can go back to the same location and repeat the performance with a total match between the virtual model and the real (it will always be necessary to verify that the settings of the projector have remained unchanged: keystone, lens shift etc.).

At this point the photograph of the facade was used, warping it to match with the colour map created. Since it was not possible to take a single photograph of the entire facade, two were taken (figure IX.6) and the overall image was rebuilt using the **Photomerge** function in Photoshop.

Figure IX.5

The result of joining the two photos, after having rectified them, is shown in figure IX.7.

Figure IX.6

Figure IX.7

After that the photo was re-sized and cleaned up as in figure IX.8 so as to make it perfectly comparable to the colour map created.

Note that the pots with flowers and the bollards have been removed with the **clone stamp** function of Photoshop (an operation which is necessary if you are sure that the items listed above will be removed or moved before the video projection).

Figure IX.8

Having concluded this phase, it is followed by a procedure which is common to all methods of mapping, ie: enhanced tracing in Illustrator, composition effects in After Effects, 3D model creation and texturing in Cinema 4D, audio video editing in Premiere and using Resolume for projection and warping.

For the facade of the church of San Gerardo Maiella di Calvi a survey was provided by the local authority but to have the perfect match of the models trace mapping was used. In fact, in figure IX.9 the model of the recreated colour maps was overlayed with the survey available and quite a few differences can be seen. If the architectural survey was used as a basis to create the mapping files, it would have been necessary to resort to warping to get a perfect match.

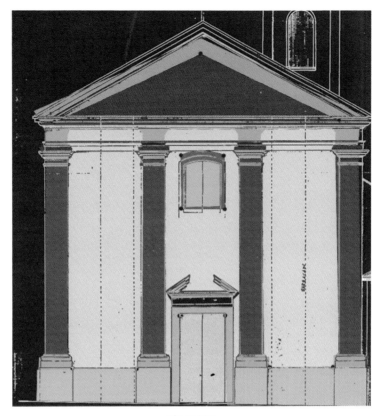

Figure IX.9

9.3 Photographic mapping

Photographic mapping, based on our experience, is the best method for most types of situation in which you have to operate. It involves the use of photography and photographic techniques of rectification of the architectural survey. Being a relatively complex method, it is recommended when the surface in addition to being very extensive is also articulated. With it you will have the texture of the facade available that can be used as the basis for the 3D model. The draft mapping does not require the use of the projector, but only the knowledge of the height and the positioning distance. To take the photo, it is not necessary to have a camera with specific features or special resolution (ideally a DSLR with standard lens, 18-55mm, because it has a wide range of shots, from wide-angle to telephoto – figure IX.10). It is useful to position it as far as possible from the subject facade so as not to introduce much distortion in the photograph.

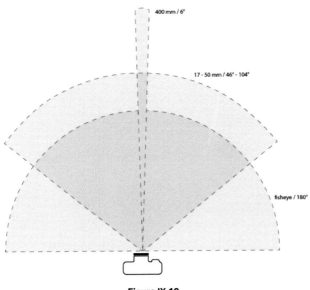

Figure IX.10

If the photo is taken at night or in low light conditions, it is advisable to use a tripod to avoid shakes and achieve a shot that is as sharp as possible. The sharpness will be crucial when, reconstructing the 3D model, the photograph itself is applied as a texture.

It is advisable to take the photo when the facade is not fully illuminated by the sun, both not to burn the whites and to avoid shadows that will be obtained later through the 3D model, so as not to interfere with those on the photograph itself. Indeed, the presence of real shadows could affect the final appearance since they would overlap with those obtained virtually.

Whenever unwanted shadows appear in the photograph, it is possible to remove them using the **clone stamp** in Photoshop.

As in the previous example, it could be necessary to take several photographs of the facade to obtain the complete image and use the **photomerge** function in Photoshop to join them. The first step for photographing architecture is to position yourself in the place calculated in advance as the position of the video projector.

To carry out photographic mapping it is necessary to know how to:

- take the photograph;
- scale the photograph;
- correct the lens blemishes;
- re-size the photograph in proportion.

How to take the photograph

When you take a photo, the axis of the camera's optical cone may be inclined relative to the horizon, and subsequently also the "frame" which includes the subject of the shot (in our case the facade) will be inclined to zenith[18].

To overcome this problem it would be better to take the photo from a height more or less central with respect to the facade and from a position as far away as possible, so as not to tilt the camera and to avoid significant optical distortions (figure IX.11).

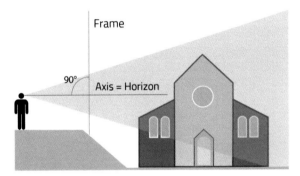 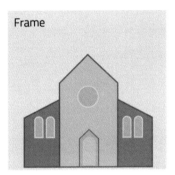

Figure IX.11

If you were forced to take the photo with the axis of the camera tilted, also the photograph would automatically be tilted with the obvious convergence of vertical perspective lines downwards (if the photograph was taken from above - figure IX.12) or upwards (if the photograph was taken from the bottom - figure IX.13).

The procedure for the correction of optical blemishes due to the lens and the inclination of the axis of the camera is defined as photographic "rectification" and consists in bringing back the vertical and horizontal lines in a parallel position between them (the frame will form an angle of 90 ° with respect to horizontal axis and is parallel to the facade) and in correcting the image so that all the elements in it come back into the right proportions.

---

18. Zenith is defined as the intersection of the perpendicular to the horizontal plane passing through the observer, with the surface of the sky visible. In this case the perpendicular passes through the centre of the camera lens.

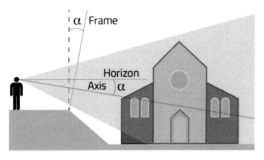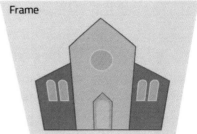

Figure IX.12

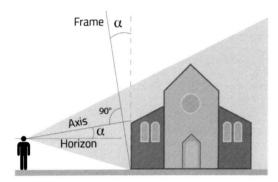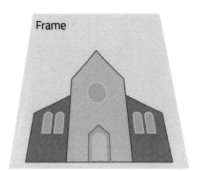

Figure IX.13

When you take a photograph it may be helpful to position on the elevation a white rod of fixed length (eg. 1 or 2 metres) to have a further reference, obviously quite rough, to put the facade in proportion.

In figure IX.14, for example, there is a photograph of the Cloister of San Francesco taken at the first edition of GLOWFestival 2013, with a SLR Canon Eos 600D, 18-55mm lens, which generated a file of 5184x3456 px 72 dpi. For the photographic rectification we recorded directly the base (21 metres) and with sextant, as described in chapter 8, the height (22 metres).

Figure IX.14

Scaling the photograph

To scale the photograph, so as to adapt it to the dimensions of the projection, you can open it in Photoshop clicking on **File > Open** and proceeding according to the steps described below:

Bring the resolution of the photograph to 72 dpi (video resolution): To check the resolution of the photograph and, if necessary, modify it, click on **Image > Image Size** (figure IX.15), and in the **Document Size** field check the value shown. If it is different from 72 Pixels/Inch (figure IX.16), replace the value with the one quoted.

Adapt the size of the photograph to the format used by the video projector: Imagine a video projector resolution of **XGA 1024x768** pixels and an **Aspect Ratio 4:3**. To adapt the photograph it is necessary, being careful that the proportions are not forced, to tick **Constrain Proportions** and go to **Image > Image Size** in the **Pixel Dimensions** field, selecting **Pixels** and in **Height** insert 768 in place of 3456 (figure IX.17).

In this way the photograph will have been re-sized to a resolution of 1152x768 pixels. An excessive value in pixels for the height was inserted, because if the value 1024 px had been inserted in the **Width**, a **Height** value equal to 683 pixels would have been obtained, as is easy to understand.

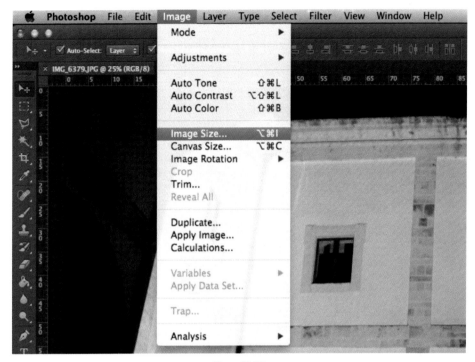

Figure IX.15

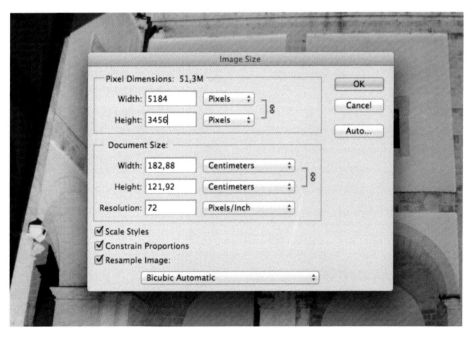

Figure IX.16

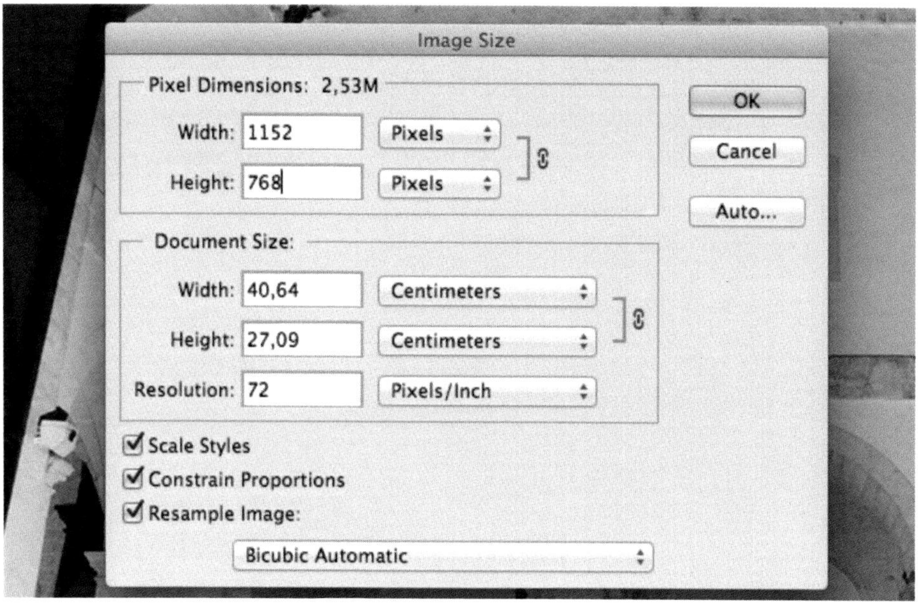

Figure IX.17

In this way, it is no longer necessary to work on the resolution of the image but simply cut the excess part of the **Canvas**. To do this, go to **Image > Canvas Size > Width** and insert the value 1024 (making sure pixels are selected). The photograph will now be in the format required. After this phase the photograph can be scaled (obtaining a black border around it) and remove all parts of the structure on which you do not want to project anything. In the mapping file the parts on left and right of the drainpipes, shadows and openings visible in the background, have been removed, trying to give the overall image uniformity and elegance.

Correcting lens blemishes, or rather: "rectifying" the photograph

After scaling the photograph, the next step is to correct the lens blemishes, proceeding to rectification. To do this, still in Photoshop, go to **Filter > Lens Correction** and open the **Custom** panel (figure IX.18).

In this phase it is useful to have the reference grid and a modification of its size and colour, so as to have further references to the vertical and horizontal lines. The parameters on which to work are **Geometric Distortion**, **Transform> Vertical Perspective** and **Scale** (figure IV.19) and they should be modified until the lines of the facade that in reality are horizontal and vertical, do not return to those in the photo, becoming parallel to the lines in the activated reference grid.

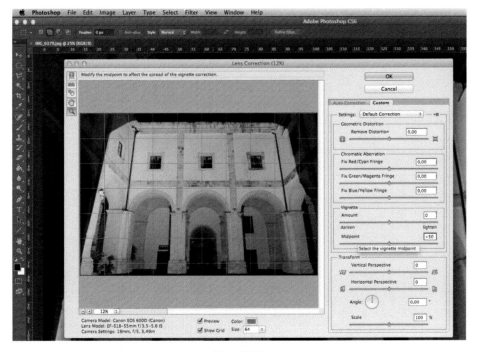

Figure IX.18

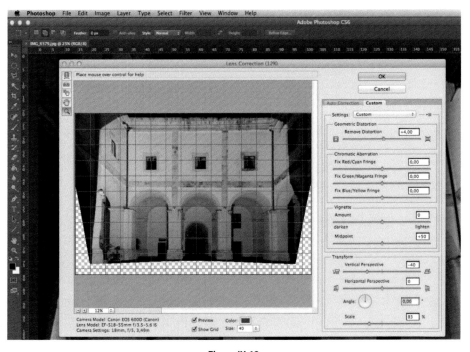

Figure IX.19

Having removed the distortion due to the lens and achieved the desired result, click **OK** to confirm the changes made. At this point the photos should be brought into the right proportions so that all the elements come back in the correct aspect ratio.

Bring the photo back in proportion

To approach the real appearance of the facade seen from the point of view of the projector, it is necessary to make adjustments according to a procedure that will enable, with a little time and practice, everything to be matched. If you do not want to carry out the method that will be illustrated, you can perform automated photographic rectification using a photo-rectification specific software that, in principle, is easy to use and at a low cost. Returning to the "manual" rectification in Photoshop, which is based on the same logic of the aforementioned software, to bring a photograph back in proportion the data at our disposal is:

- Resolution XGA - 1024x768 pixels; Aspect Ratio 1024/768=4/3=1,3 recurring;
- Base of the building (b=21 m) and height (h=22 m) in which the ratio (21/22) is 0,95.

Measure the base of the building on the screen by using the **Rectangle shape tool** after having chosen pixels as the unit of measurement in **Preferences > Units & Rulers** (figure IX.20). In the moment when the base rectangle is drawn, the value of the Width in pixels appears, for which 21 m equal to 748 pixels should be entered.

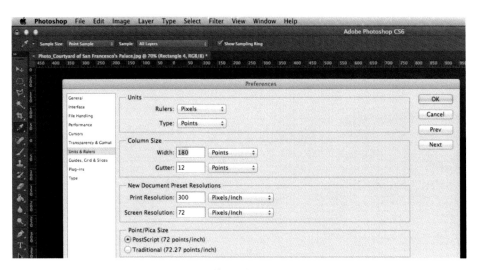

Figure IX.20

Since when you take a photograph (from above or below) the value that suffers the greatest distortion is the height, putting the photo in proportion needs to act precisely on this dimension.

To know what should be the value of the height in pixels, just a simple proportion in which the known factors are the base in metres, the correspondence of it in pixels and the height in metres. To determine the value of the height in pixels y:

$$21 \text{ m} : 748 \text{ pixel} = 22 \text{ m} : y \text{ pixel}$$

$$y = (748*22)/21 = 783,6 \text{ px}$$

Having defined the height, a rectangle can be drawn with its Height value equal to 783,6 pixels and using the functions **Edit > Transform > Scale** and/or **Distort** in Photoshop everything can be brought back in proportion by distorting the image until the height coincides with the constraints imposed by the measures introduced by the rectangle used as reference.

To assess the measurements after having constructed the rectangle, simply press A on the keyboard and select the related rectangle of which you want to know the measurements in pixels (figure IX.21).

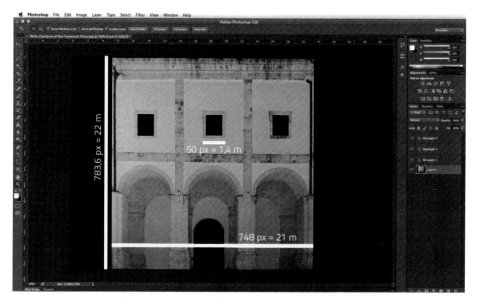

Figure IX.21

Knowing a measurement in pixels, always through proportion, we can know its value in metres. For example if an element x on the screen measures 50 px (the base of the center window) to "convert" the value into metres just use the above procedure and therefore:

$$x = (21*50)/748 = 1,40 \text{ m}$$

Taking back into Photoshop a couple of measurements of real items recorded directly (width and height of windows, arches, doors etc.) we can distort the photo until those elements are not the right size. Finally, the file was cleaned up as in figure IX.21.

The image, scalable without its proportions being altered, will be taken as an absolute starting point of the whole workflow described in chapter 3 onwards.

Once the desired result is achieved, the image can be saved in the **.jpg** format by clicking on **File > Save As**.

It should be emphasised that in this step any excessive precision is not necessary since further distortions can be carried out in the process of warping.

Chapter 10

Procedure for implementing
a video mapping event

Art does not reproduce what is visible,
it makes things visible.

Paul Klee

Lyric Globers,
Video mapping
performance
off contest,
GLOWFestival First
edition, Cloister of
San Frnacesco, Ostui
(BR), 2013

CHAPTER 10

10.1 Video mapping and bureacracy

The organisation of a video mapping event includes some bureaucratic paperwork that can vary depending on the country and the place in which the event has been programmed. In this volume the bureaucratic process to follow in Italy is described and it is based on the hypothesis of an event to be organised in a location where only one body is involved, the Council. The first step is to enquire at the Public Relations Office as to what the process to follow is. Whether or not a request to occupy public property temporarily can be onerous depends on the Council to which you make the enquiry. In addition to the request of permission/authorisation, you will certainly need to prepare a photographic survey of the area.

Usually the person who has the responsibility of requesting the necessary permits is the client, but of course a lot depends on the specific agreements made between the client and the organiser of the video mapping event. In any case it would be at least expected that the client repay the expenses incurred by the organiser for fulfilling the paperwork. In this respect it is important that in the letter of professional engagement, which is a kind of handbook of rules between the event organiser and client, the duties and charges due to each part are well specified.

In general the permits to be requested are: the authorisation for the projection, permission for the occupation of public property, permission for the temporary switching off of public lighting and permission to close the area.

Lyric Globers,
Video mapping
performance
off contest,
GLOWFestival
First edition,
Cloister of
San Frnacesco,
Ostui (BR),
2013

Authorisation for the video projection

The authorisation for the video projection is a permit issued in written form and it must be requested from the owner of the property on which the projection will be made. In the permit the owner must authorise the screening and indicate the number of days and the times when video projections are allowed.

Permission for the occupation of public property

The permit to occupy public property is an authorisation that is requested for two occasions: for mapping the facade and for the performance. The request for the permit must be attached to a plan showing the overall dimensions provided in square metres. This amount will be used to calculate the relative fee for the occupation of public property required by most Councils.

Typically for the calculation of the area occupied, the dimensions of the scaffolding supporting the projector, the workstation, the power generator and speakers will be added.

In some cases the audio/video service must certify that they comply with safety guidelines.

Permission for temporarily switching off the public lighting

Permission for switching off the public lighting temporarily, like that the of the occupation of public property, is also required for both the date of the mapping and the date of the performance. The request for the permit must be attached to a plan which sets out the street lights which require switching off, making sure to include the codes on the label (adhesive or metal) of each lamppost.

At the time of the request it is necessary to ensure that the Council, once permission is granted, give notice to the Police or other bodies of the temporary switching off of the public lighting so that they, for reasons of public security, can be deployed in the area concerned during the performance and, if they think fit, a larger number of police.

In the case that the Council does not inform the Police, it could mean that one of them, feeling that the performance is a risk to public order, can block it.

Permission to close the area

In the request for closure of an area, normally addressed to the Council or the Police, it is necessary to attach a plan carrying the layout of the closure that will be required to guarantee the security of the equipment, performers and people that could gather near to the workstation.

In the following paragraphs are examples of the requests for permits usable as templates for video mapping performances. Such templates are based on the requests sent by the gloWArp studio to the Council of Canosa di Puglia (BT), Italy, for the performance made in August 2012 on the facade of the Cathedral of San Sabino located there (figure X.1).

Figure X.1 – Cathedral of San Sabino, Canosa di Puglia (BT) – Italy.

10.2 Request for authorisation of the video projection

For the attention of ....

proprietor of ....

located in ....

Subject: Request for authorisation of a video projection on the facade of the building.

The undersigned .... born at .... on .... and resident at ....
tel. .... as legal representative of Company / Association, etc.

REQUESTS

the authorisation of the video projection on the facade of the building owned by you in
.... on the following days and times: ....

DECLARES

to respect the provisions of the municipal planning rules and that, being exclusively of video projections, the facade will not be in any way compromised.

ATTACHES (if requested or considered appropriate)

- *Draft of the project with the area of the performance indicated.*

Town, ... / ...... / ....   Yours faithfully

                                    ....

10.3 Request for occupation of public property

For the attention of the Council ....

Subject: Request for permission of the temporary occupation of public property.

The undersigned .... born at .... on .... and resident at .... tel. .... as legal representative of Company / Association, etc.

REQUESTS

to occupy temporarily with the following elements:

- scaffolding for the video projector

- workstation

- power generator

- speakers

the area of Council property (as indicated on the attached photographic survey) located in ...., of space equal to .... m², for the following days and times: ....

DECLARES

to respect until the end of the occupation of public property located in ...., the provisions of the municipal planning rules and to be open to pay, where applicable, the cost of the permit.

ATTACHES

- *Plan showing the area to be occupied (figure X.2).*

- *Declaration of conformity of the audio/electrical equipment.*

Town, ... /...... /............   Yours faithfully

....

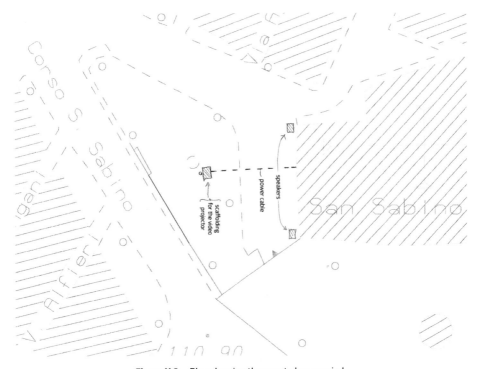

Figure X.2 – Plan showing the area to be occupied.

10.4 Request for the authorisation to switch off the public lighting temporarily

For the attention of the Council ....

Subject: Request for the authorisation to switch off the public lighting temporarily

The undersigned...............born at.................on...........and resident at....................................
tel. .... as legal respresentative of Company / Association, etc.

DECLARES

that on the date .... an architectural video projection performance, also called video mapping, will take place, on the facade of ....

FOR THIS REASON REQUESTS,

for a successful outcome of the event, the switching off of the street lights listed below (see attached plan) (figure X.3) on the days and at the hours listed below:

List of street lights:
1) 19029, 2) 19030, 3) 19031, 4) 19032, 5) 19033, 6) 19034, 7) 19035, 8) 19036, 9) 19037, 10) 19038, 11) 19039, 12) 19041, 13) 19042, 14) 19043, 15) 19044, 16) 19045, 17) 19046, 18) 19047, 19) 19048, 20) 14001, 21) 14002, 22) 17008, 23) 17009, 24) 20001, 25) 44064, 26) 44065

Days and times: ....

FURTHERMORE DECLARES,

given the number of the remaining street lamps that would stay lit, that the switching off of these lights will never leave the square completely dark and the projector will remain in operation during the hours for which the shutdown is required ensuring, in replacement of the street lights switched off, an alternative light source that still offers a good overall brightness of the space that is the subject of the projection.

ATTACHES

- *Plan showing the area of the performance*

Town, ... / ...... / ....   Yours faithfully

....

Figure X.3 – Plan showing the street lights to be switched off.

10.5 Request for the closure of the area

For the attention of the Council ....

Subject: Request for the closure of an area to prevent pedestrian access

The undersigned .... born at .... on .... and resident at .... tel. .... as legal representative of Company/Association, etc.

REQUESTS

Permission to temporarily close an area of Council property located in .... for an architectural video projection performance, also called video mapping, which will take place on .... for the following days and times...................................... .

DECLARES

to respect until the end of the occupation of public property located in ...., the provisions of the municipal planning rules and to be open to pay, where applicable, the cost of the permit.

ATTACHES

- *Plan showing the area of the performance (figure X.4).*

Town, ... /...... /............   Yours faithfully

                                        ....

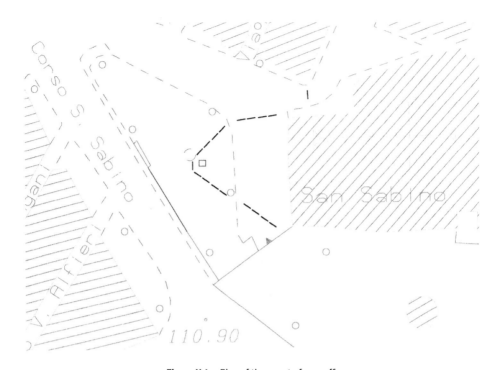

Figure X.4 – Plan of the area to fence off.